THE ORIGAMI GARDEN

PERFECTLY MINDFUL ORIGAMI

THE ORIGAMI GARDEN

MARK BOLITHO

jacqui small

First published in 2017 by
Jacqui Small LLP
74–77 White Lion Street
London N1 9PF

Publisher: Jacqui Small
Managing Editor: Emma Heyworth-Dunn
Commissioning and Project Editor: Joanna Copestick
Senior Designer: Rachel Cross
Assistant Designer: Clare Thorpe
Photography: Brent Darby
Production: Maeve Healy

ISBN: 978-1-911127-10-9

A catalogue record for this book is available
from the British Library.

2019 2018 2017
10 9 8 7 6 5 4 3 2 1

Printed in China

Scaling and Sizes

Each project is accompanied by a scaling
diagram that shows the size of the final
model compared to the starting sheet of
paper. The diagram is based on a square
sheet with dimensions of 18 x 18cm (7 x 7in),
or an equivalent rectangle. However, larger
or smaller models can be made. The size of
the final model can be scaled up or down by
comparing the dimensions of the paper used
to the sheet used in the scaling diagram.

Complexity Ratings

The projects in this book have been given a
rating based on their complexity. They appear
beneath the title of each project.

Easy ✳

Intermediate ✳✳

More Challenging ✳✳✳

Quarto is the authority on a wide range of topics.
Quarto educates, entertains and enriches the lives of
our readers – enthusiasts and lovers of hands-on living.
www.QuartoKnows.com

CONTENTS

MINDFUL ORIGAMI

Welcome to the world of origami, the art of paper folding. At its heart it is the transformation of a sheet of paper into a finished model. However, it's not only a matter of creating a finished model, but also a journey of paper folding that involves creativity and contemplation along the way to produce your finished piece of work.

The word 'origami' comes from the Japanese word for paper folding. In the East the craft developed based on standard forms and traditional designs and it now has many enthusiasts around the world.

The Internet has enabled the sharing of ideas and lead to a collective enthusiasm for developing more beautiful and complex designs. In the chase for complexity, however, some of the beauty of the craft has been overlooked. This is a discrepancy I hope to overcome with this book, by presenting mindful finished works in appropriate colours and compositions.

The paper-folding process can be a contemplative journey, Over time a plain sheet of paper is transformed into something wonderful. The satisfaction of origami comes not only from creating interesting designs, but also from following the folding journey and seeing your model evolve at your fingertips. Origami offers a perfect way to explore your mindful creativity in the colours and paper choices you use. In addition, you can explore and consider the nature of paper itself and the final composition of groups of complementary models.

The projects in this collection have been selected based on the aesthetic quality of the final model and the folding processes. They are explained with step-by-step diagrams that show the sequences needed to produce the final design.

At the start of the collection I have included instructions for the Easy Rose (see page 10). This is an opportunity to gain familiarity with the diagrams and symbols used to explain the folding sequences. Some models are more complex than others and we have given a rating to each project as a guide (see page 4).

If you are new to origami, try starting with the easier models and working up to the more complex projects.I hope you enjoy folding these projects as much as I enjoyed designing them.

GETTING STARTED

Here are the basic folding techniques and symbols you'll need to complete the projects in the book.

FOLDING IN HALF

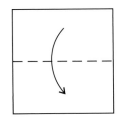 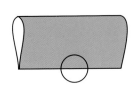 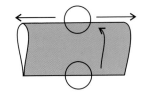 

1. The step indicates that the paper should be folded in half.

2. First of all line up the opposite sides of the paper and hold the edges together.

3. When the two layers are aligned, pinch the middle to hold them together. Then make the crease.

4. The paper is accurately folded in half.

ARROWS AND FOLDS

Paper-folding instructions explain the folding process with a series of steps leading to a finished model. Each step explains one or two folds in the process. Steps should be followed in order and when a step is completed, it should resemble the image shown in the next step.

The transition from one step to the next is shown by a series of lines and arrows indicating where folds should be made. The lines show where to fold and the arrows show how the paper should be moved to make folds.

Folds are described as either Mountain Folds or Valley Folds.

These names refer to how the surface will look after the fold has been completed. A Mountain Fold will fold towards the observer, forming a mountain shape, while the Valley Fold will fold away, forming a V or valley shape. They are represented by differing dotted-line symbols.

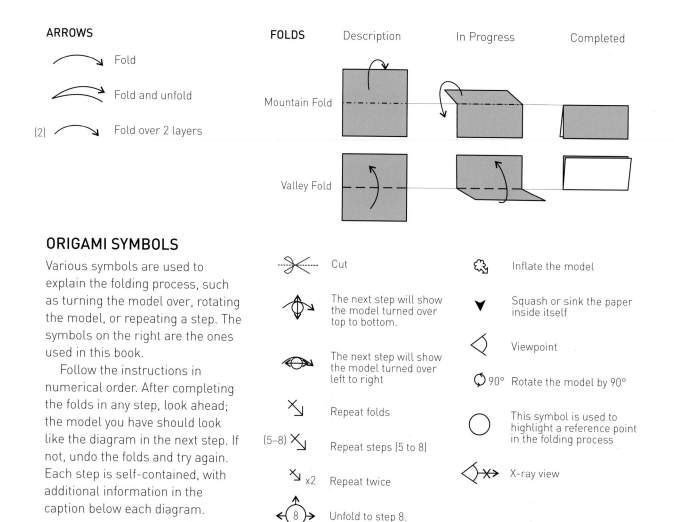

ARROWS

— Fold

— Fold and unfold

(2) — Fold over 2 layers

FOLDS   Description   In Progress   Completed

Mountain Fold

Valley Fold

ORIGAMI SYMBOLS

Various symbols are used to explain the folding process, such as turning the model over, rotating the model, or repeating a step. The symbols on the right are the ones used in this book.

Follow the instructions in numerical order. After completing the folds in any step, look ahead; the model you have should look like the diagram in the next step. If not, undo the folds and try again. Each step is self-contained, with additional information in the caption below each diagram.

✂ Cut

⊕ The next step will show the model turned over top to bottom.

👁 The next step will show the model turned over left to right

⟍ Repeat folds

(5–8) ⟍ Repeat steps (5 to 8)

⟍ x2 Repeat twice

←(8)→ Unfold to step 8.

🐾 Inflate the model

▼ Squash or sink the paper inside itself

◁ Viewpoint

↻ 90° Rotate the model by 90°

○ This symbol is used to highlight a reference point in the folding process

◇→ X-ray view

DIAGRAMS

The diagrams are shown in two colours, with the coloured side being the front and the white side being the reverse. This should make the step-by-step instructions easier to follow.

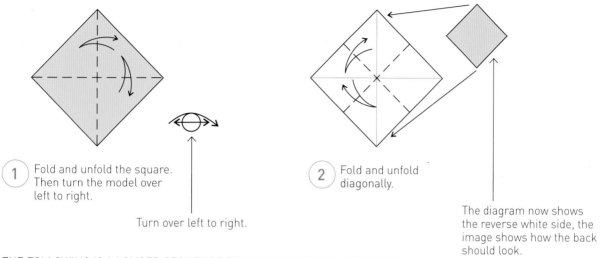

1. Fold and unfold the square. Then turn the model over left to right.

Turn over left to right.

2. Fold and unfold diagonally.

The diagram now shows the reverse white side, the image shows how the back should look.

THE FOLLOWING IS A LONGER SEQUENCE TO MAKE A PRELIMINARY BASE.

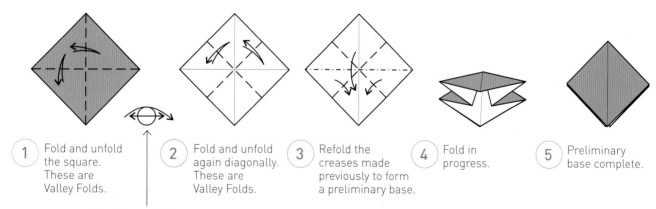

1. Fold and unfold the square. These are Valley Folds.

Turn the model over.

2. Fold and unfold again diagonally. These are Valley Folds.

3. Refold the creases made previously to form a preliminary base.

4. Fold in progress.

5. Preliminary base complete.

Origami instructions take you through a step-by-step process from start to finish. Symbols are included to explain the transition from one step to the next. Each step shows how the folded project should look and shows the folds that should be applied to progress to the next step.

When approaching a step, do look ahead to the next diagram to see how the model should look when the fold has been applied. Then check and make sure that the paper model you are making resembles the step diagram.

Look out for reference points to compare your model with the instructions to make sure. you remain on the right track.

If your model doesn't resemble the step you are on, unfold the last step and work back until it does.

Easy Rose

*

The rose is made from a few simple folds and is included to introduce some of the symbols used in this book. The model works by folding a series of layers that become the petals of the flower. It has simple lines and an elegant simplicity.

18 X 18CM (7 X 7IN)

x1

B 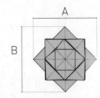 A

A 9.5cm (3¾in)
B 9.5cm (3¾in)

START WITH A SQUARE, COLOURED SIDE DOWN.

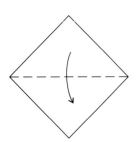
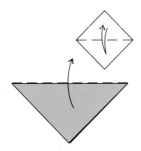
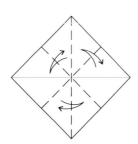
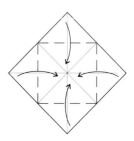

(1) Fold the paper in half diagonally.

(2) Unfold. This process (steps 1–2), can be represented by an up and down arrow.

(3) Fold and unfold the square in half length-wise and diagonally along all axes.

(4) Fold the corners in to the middle.

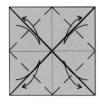
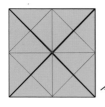
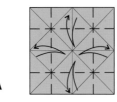
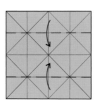

(5) Fold and unfold the corners in to the middle.

(6) Turn the model over left to right.

(7) Fold and unfold the outer edges in to the middle on all sides.

(8) Fold the upper and lower edges in to the middle.

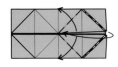
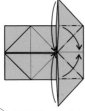
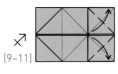

(9) Fold the right side in, open out the section and squash it flat.

(10) Fold the points up perpendicular to the base, separate the layers and squash flat.

(11) Fold the corners out. Then repeat steps 9 to 11 on the left side of the paper.

(12) Turn the model over left to right.

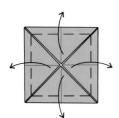
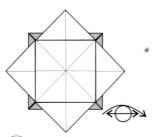
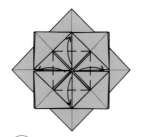
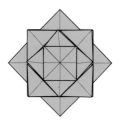

(13) Fold the corners out on all sides.

(14) Turn the model over left to right.

(15) Fold the corners in the middle section out.

(16) Complete.

SEEDS AND PLANTS

Seeds

A seed is a good start for any garden. The model works well across a group, perhaps in different colours to represent different types. You could also experiment with making seeds from paper patterns of the plants and flowers they will become.

9 X 9CM (3½ X 3½IN)

A 3cm (1¼in)
B 6.5cm (2½in)
C 0.5cm (¼in)

START WITH A SQUARE, COLOURED SIDE UP.

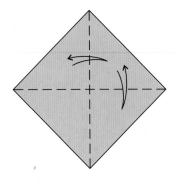

1 Fold and unfold the square in half diagonally along both axes.

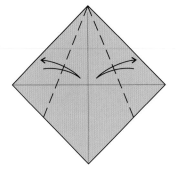

2 Fold and unfold the edges into the middle crease.

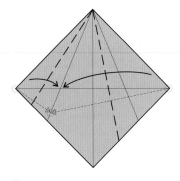

3 Fold the outer edges so that both outer edges touch the crease made previously.

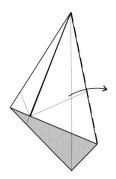

4 Unfold the right side.

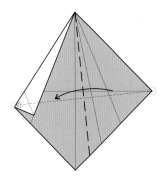

5 Fold the side over to enable the outer edge to touch the opposite folded edge.

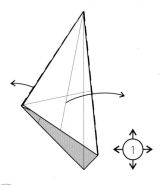

6 Unfold back to a square.

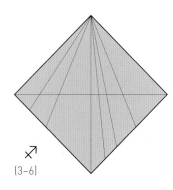

(3–6)

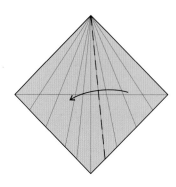

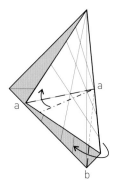

7 Repeat steps 3 to 6 on the other side of the paper.

8 Fold one side over along the crease adjacent to middle.

9 Fold the lower section up along (a–a). This will cause the lower edge (a–b) to fold in.

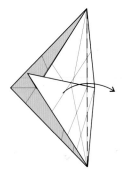

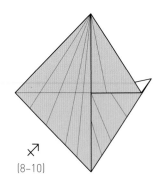

(8–10)

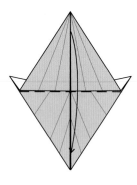

10 Fold the section over.

11 Repeat steps 8 to 10 on the other side of the paper.

12 Fold the upper section down along the middle.

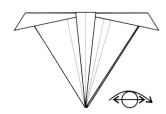

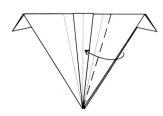

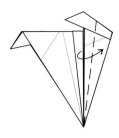

13 Turn the paper over left to right.

14 Fold the right side in. The outer edge should touch the middle crease.

15 Fold both layers of the folded section out, aligned with the edge of the middle section.

16 Fold the upper edge of the model over and in to the middle crease.

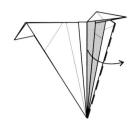

17 Fold the whole section over.

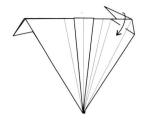

18 Fold the outer corner over.

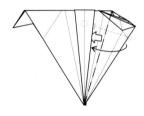

19 Fold the section over and tuck the edge into the middle section.

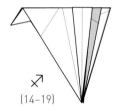

(14–19)

20 Repeat steps 14 to 19 on the other side of the paper.

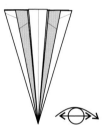

21 Turn the paper over left to right.

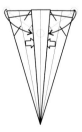

22 Fold the upper corners in and tuck them beneath the edges of the middle section.

23 Turn the paper over left to right.

24 Complete.

Nuts in a Bowl
**

The nut shows how straight folds can be combined to make a suggestion of texture and curves. Although most nuts are brown, try experimenting with different coloured and patterned papers to make more exotic varieties as you explore your creativity.

18 X 18CM (7 X 7IN)

x1

A

B

C

A 5.5cm (2¼in)
B 8cm (3in)
C 5.5cm (2¼in)

x1

A

B

C

A 14cm (5½in)
B 3cm (1¼in)
C 14cm (5½in)

START WITH A SQUARE, COLOURED SIDE UP.

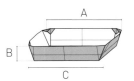
Fold in progress.

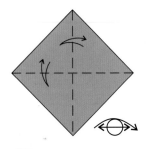

① Fold and unfold the square in half diagonally along both axes. Then turn the paper over left to right.

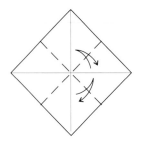

② Fold and unfold the square lengthwise along both axes.

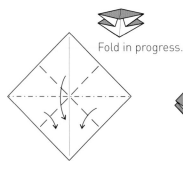

③ Fold the upper half down. At the same time fold in the sides, making a preliminary base.

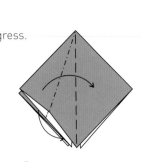

④ Fold the corner up, separate the layers and squash flat.

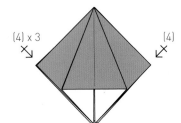

(4) x 3   (4)

⑤ Squash the other three corners repeating step 4.

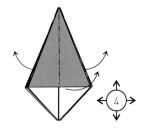

(4)

⑥ Fold out the squashed sides back to a preliminary base.

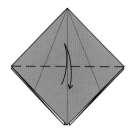

⑦ Fold and unfold along the middle of the square.

⑧ Repeat from upper corner to middle crease.

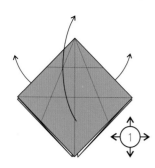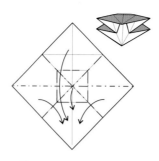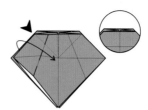

(9) Open out the model back to a square.

(10) Refold the model and reverse the middle section inside along the creases made in step 8.

(11) Fold one side up, perpendicular to the model. Separate the layers and squash flat.

(12) Fold one layer back over.

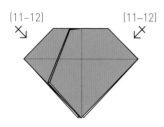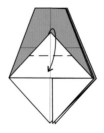

(13) Repeat steps 11 to 12 on the other three corners.

(14) Fold the lower corner up.

(15) Fold the corner down to the adjacent folded edge.

(16) Fold the upper layer back down again.

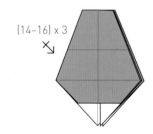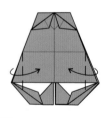

(17) Repeat steps 14 to 16 on the other three sides.

(18) Fold the right side over.

(19) Fold the two upper and two lower corners in.

(20) Fold the side edges in.

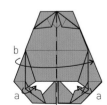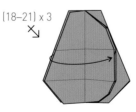

(21) Fold (a) in to create the nut. Fold one side over to the right (b).

(22) Repeat steps 18 to 21 on the other three faces

(23) Separate the layers and give the nut some shape.

(24) Complete.

MAKING THE BOWL

START WITH STEPS 1–3 OF THE SEEDLING POT ON PAGE 22.

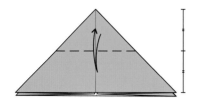

1. Fold and unfold the upper corner down to the middle crease.

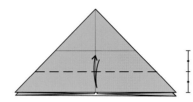

2. Fold the lower edge up to the crease made previously, then unfold.

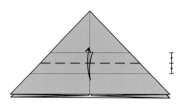

3. Fold and unfold between the creases.

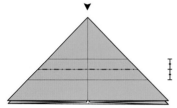

4. Sink the upper corner into the model along the crease made in step 3.

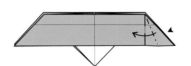

5. Fold up the right corner perpendicular to the model and squash flat.

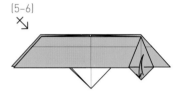

(5–6)

6. Fold and unfold the corner. Then repeat steps 5 to 6 on the other three corners.

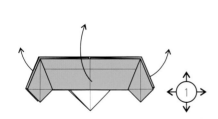

7. Unfold back to a square.

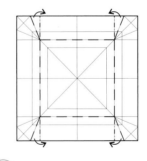

8. Fold the corners in slightly.

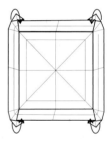

9. Fold the corners over.

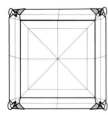

10. Fold the corners over again to shape the edge.

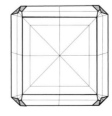

11. Crease the edges of the model to shape the bowl.

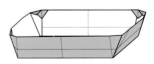

12. Complete.

Seedlings in a Pot

✱✱

As the seed begins to grow, the seedling will start to sprout. These models form a series, starting from the first shoot to the leaves appearing. Symbolizing new life and growth, this composite model is a good introduction to the plants that follow later in the book.

18 X 18CM (7 X 7IN)
1 X BLUE, 1 X TAN,
1 X GREEN

 x3

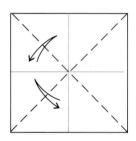

A 7.5cm (3in)
B 14cm (5in)
C 7.5cm (3in)
D 6.5 cm (2½in)

TO MAKE THE POT START WITH A SQUARE, COLOURED SIDE UP.

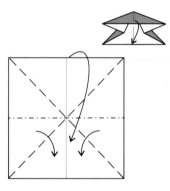

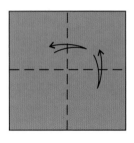

1 Fold and unfold the square in half lengthwise along both axes. Then turn the paper over left to right.

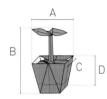

2 Fold and unfold the square diagonally along both axes.

3 Fold the upper edge down. At the same time refold the creases made previously. This is called a waterbomb base.

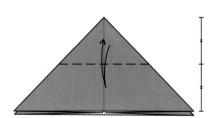

4 Fold and unfold the upper corner down to form a middle crease.

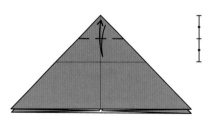

5 Fold and unfold the upper corner into the crease made previously.

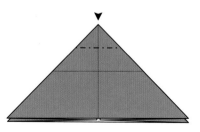

6 Sink-fold the upper corner into the model. This process will be shown in the next two steps.

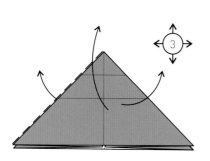

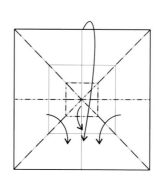

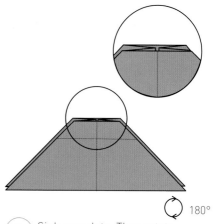

180°

(7) Unfold back to a square.

(8) Refold the waterbomb base (step 3) and reverse fold the inner square into the model.

(9) Sink complete. Then rotate the model by 180°.

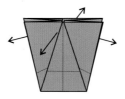

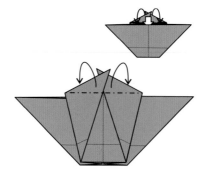

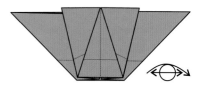

(10) Fold the sides in as indicated.

(11) Fold the corners behind.

(12) Turn the model over left to right.

(10–11)

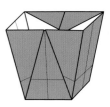

(13) Repeat steps 10 to 11.

(14) Open out the model.

(15) Pot complete.

EARTH FOR THE POT

START WITH A SQUARE, COLOURED SIDE, UP AND FOLLOW STEPS 1-11 OF THE NUTS IN A BOWL (SEE PAGES 18-20).

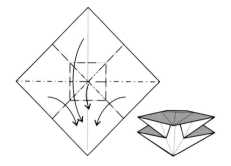 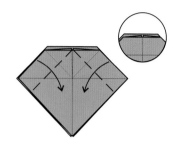 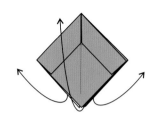 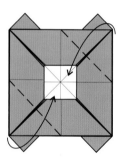 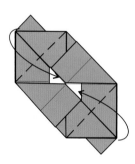

1. Fold the preliminary base back together and reverse fold in the middle square.

2. Fold the sides in.

3. Fold the upper section up and open out the model.

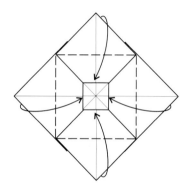

4. Fold the corners in and tuck them under the middle section.

5. Fold the upper right and lower left corners in.

6. Fold the other two corners in.

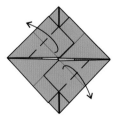 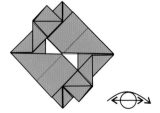 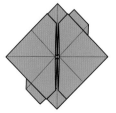

7. Fold the upper layers out again where indicated.

8. Turn the model over left to right.

9. Earth complete.

TO MAKE THE SEEDLING START WITH A SQUARE, COLOURED SIDE DOWN.

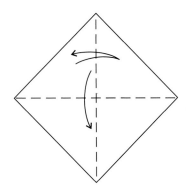

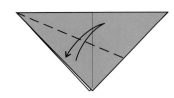

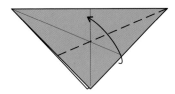

1. Fold the square in half diagonally, then fold the upper corner down.

2. Fold two layers up to touch upper folded edge. Unfold

3. Fold two layers up to touch the upper edge.

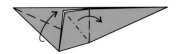

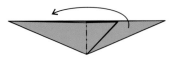

4. Fold the edge over and refold the creases made previously.

5. Fold the right point behind.

6. Fold the left corner of the upper layer over. Then turn the model over left to right.

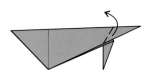

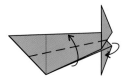

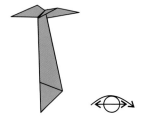

7. Fold the corner to be perpendicular to the model.

8. Fold the lower edge up to the upper edge. Then rotate the model.

9. Turn the model over left to right.

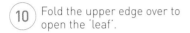

10 Fold the upper edge over to open the 'leaf'.

11 Fold the lower section up.

12 Open the point and squash flat.

13 Rotate the base to be perpendicular to the model.

14 Fold in the edge of the corner.

15 Pinch the 'stalk' to narrow the model.

16 Seedling complete.

TO ASSEMBLE

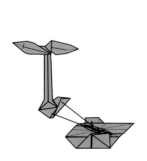

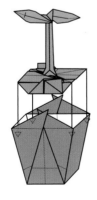

1 Insert seedling into the earth.

2 Place the assembly into the flower pot.

3 Fold the edges of the pot over into the earth.

4 Complete.

Plants in Pots

✳✳

The leaf and stalk are the first elements of a plant system that will enable you to develop your own origami pot plants. Leaves can be slotted into the stalk and added as the plant grows, then a variety of flowers (see pages 37–47) can be added.

18 X 18CM (7 X 7IN) x1

A
B
C

A 8.5cm (3⅓in)
B 5.5cm (2in)
C 8.5cm (3⅓in)

START WITH A SQUARE, COLOURED SIDE UP, AND FOLLOW STEPS 1 TO 8 OF THE CLASSIC LILY (SEE PAGES 64-6).

(1) Rotate the model by 180°.

(2) Fold the sides in at a slight angle.

(3) Fold one side over, front and back, to expose an unfolded face.

(2–3) x 3

(4) Repeat steps 2 to 3 on the other three faces.

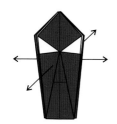

(5) Open out the model and shape the base.

(6) Fold the corners in on each side.

(7) Fold the sections over again to sit perpendicular to the edge of the bowl.

(8) Complete.

POT FILLING TAKE A SECOND SQUARE TO PRODUCE A FILLING FOR THE POT.
FOLD A PRELIMINARY BASE BY FOLLOWING STEPS 1 TO 3 OF THE NUT (PAGE 18).

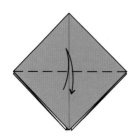

Fold in progress.

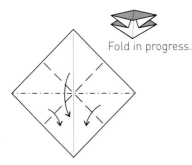

(1) Fold the upper half down. At the same time fold in the sides making a preliminary base.

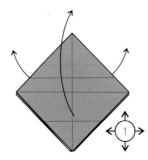

(2) Fold and unfold the model in half.

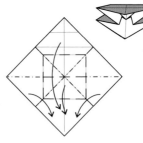

(3) Fold the lower corner up to touch the crease made in step 2 previously, and unfold.

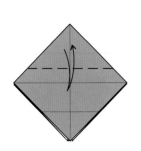

(4) Fold the upper corner down to touch the crease made previously in step 3..

(5) Unfold the model back to a square.

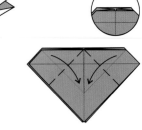

(6) Refold the preliminary base and reverse fold the inner section.

(7) Fold the outer corners in, front and back.

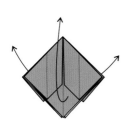

(8) Open out and flatten the model.

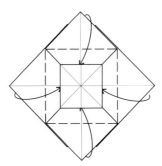

(9) Fold the corners in and tuck them under the middle square.

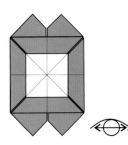

(10) Turn the model over left to right.

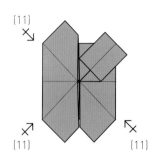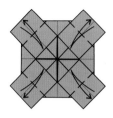

11 Fold the upper right corner up, separate the layers and squash the section flat.

12 Repeat step 11 on the other three corners.

13 Fold the corners in to the adjacent square. The next step will show the model at a different angle.

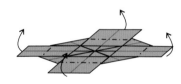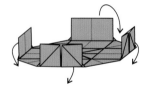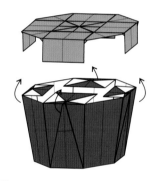

14 Fold the outer edges up so they are perpendicular to the model.

15 Fold them down again so they are perpendiclar to the model.

16 Fold the flaps around the edge of the plant pot up.

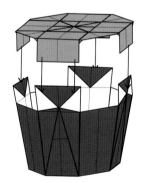

17 Insert the tabs in the 'earth' section into the tabs around the edge of the plant pot.

18 Push the inner section inside the plant pot.

19 Complete.

TRUNK

START WITH A SQUARE, COLOURED SIDE UP.

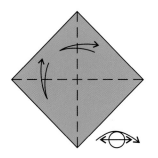

1. Fold and unfold the square in half diagonally. Then turn the paper over left to right.

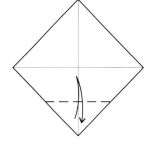

2. Fold and unfold the lower corner up to touch middle crease.

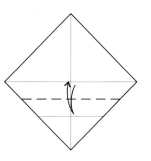

3. Fold and unfold between the creases made previously.

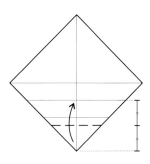

4. Fold the lower corner up to the crease made in step 3.

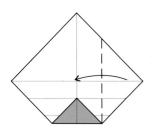

5. Fold the right side to the edge of the folded-in corner.

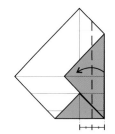

6. Fold the edge over again, aligning it with the middle.

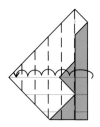

7. Fold the edge over repeatedly and roll up the paper.

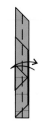

8. Fold and unfold along the middle.

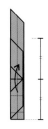

9. Fold the lower section up.

10. Pinch the upper section together and fold down to the right.

11. Fold the section back to the left and stand the upper section perpendicular to the base.

12. Trunk complete.

BRANCH

FOR A LARGER BRANCH, USE A FULL-SIZE SQUARE, COLOURED SIDE UP. FOR A SMALLER BRANCH, USE A SQUARE THAT IS A QUARTER OF THE SIZE AND FOLLOW THE INSTRUCTIONS UNTIL STEP 7.

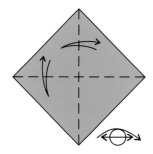

(1) Fold and unfold the square in half diagonally along both axes. Then turn the paper over left to right.

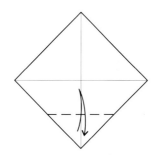

(2) Fold and unfold the lower corner to the middle.

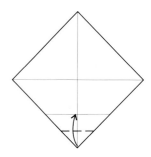

(3) Fold the lower corner up to the crease made in step 2.

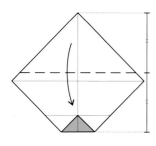

(4) Fold the upper section down to the lower folded edge.

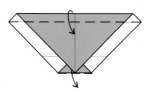

(5) Fold upper section over then fold down the lower corner.

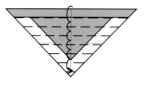

(6) Fold the same section down and roll up the paper.

(7) Fold the right side over in to the left.

(8) Fold the model in half.

(9) Complete.

LEAF

START WITH A SQUARE, COLOURED SIDE UP. THE SQUARE SHOULD
BE A THIRD OF THE WIDTH OF THAT USED FOR THE BRANCH.

BRANCH 18CM (7IN)

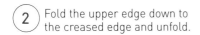

LEAF 6CM (2 ⅜IN)

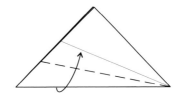

1 Fold the lower section up
along the middle.

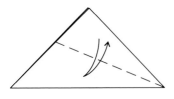

2 Fold the upper edge down to
the creased edge and unfold.

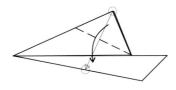

3 Fold the lower edge up to the
adjacent crease.

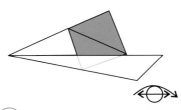

4 Fold the upper corner over
and beneath the folded lower
section.

5 Turn the model over left
to right.

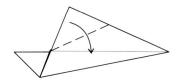

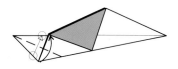

6 Fold the corner over.

7 Fold the edge of the outer corner up to touch the folded edge above.

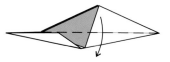

8 Fold the corner in half to further narrow the stalk.

9 Fold the upper section down.

10 Pinch and curl the 'stalk'.

11 Complete.

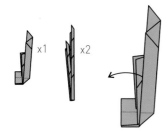
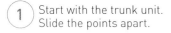

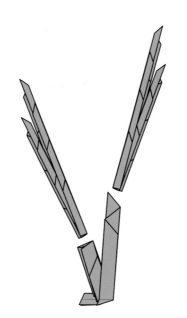

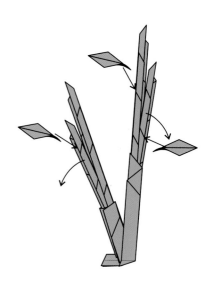

1. Start with the trunk unit. Slide the points apart.

2. Insert branch units into each section of the trunk.

3. Bend the stalks to shape the plant. Add more units for a bigger plant. Then insert the leaves into the branch; the tip of the 'stalk' should slide beneath the edge of the paper.

4. Add more leaves and insert the base of the plant into the centre of the plant pot.

5. Add flowers (see pages 37–47) by inserting their stalks within the layers.

6. Model complete.

Flowers

This section features a collection of flowers, made from squares and later pentagons, which can be added to complete the pot plants. These projects allow for experimentation, as new branches and flowers can be added over time.

A. Hydrangea flower
B. Four-petal blossom flower
C. Four-petal balloon flower
D. Five-petal blossom flower
E Five-petal balloon flower

Hydrangea Flower *

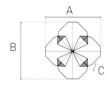

A 13.5cm (5⅓in)
B 13.5cm (5⅓in)
C 6.75cm (2½in)

x1

18 X 18CM (7 X 7IN)

START WITH A SQUARE, COLOURED SIDE UP.

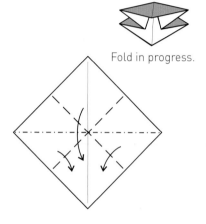

Fold in progress.

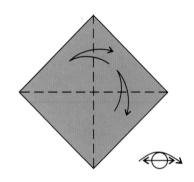

(1) Fold and unfold the square in half diagonally. Then turn the paper over left to right.

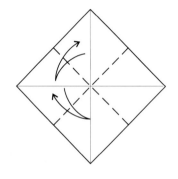

(2) Fold and unfold along the paper lengthwise.

(3) Fold the upper section down and fold the outer corners in, making a preliminary base.

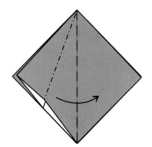

(4) Fold the corner up, separate the layers and squash flat.

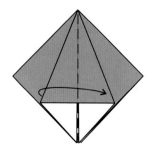

(5) Fold one layer to the right to expose the adjacent face.

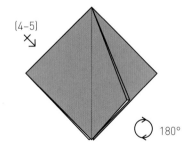

(4–5)

180°

(6) Repeat steps 4 to 5 on the other three faces. Then rotate the model by 180°.

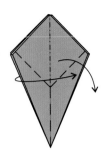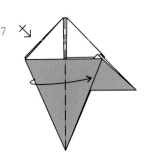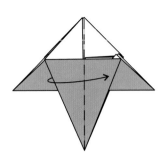

7 Fold the upper section down to lie perpendicular to the model. At the same time fold the edge over to the right.

8 Fold over three layers and repeat step 7 on the left side.

9 Fold the side back over.

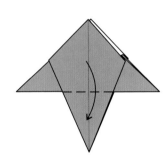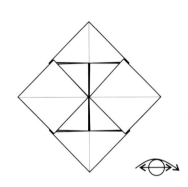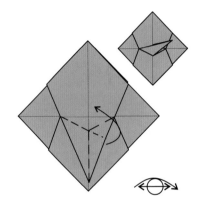

10 Fold the upper section down.

11 Turn the model over left to right

12 Pinch the two sides of the stalk together and fold it up. Then turn the model over.

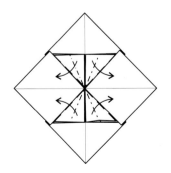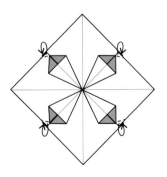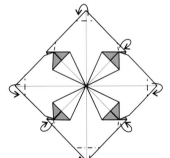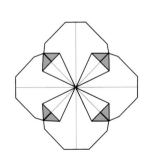

13 Fold the inner triangles up, separate the layers and squash flat.

14 Reverse fold the tips of the corners inside to start to shape the petals.

15 Fold the corners in to continue shaping the petals.

16 Complete.

Four-petal Blossom Flower **

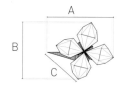

A 6.5cm (2½in)
B 6.5cm (2½in)
C 6cm (2⅓in)

x1

18 X 18CM (7 X 7IN)

START WITH A SQUARE, COLOURED SIDE UP,
AND FOLLOW STEPS 1 TO 3 ON PAGE 38.

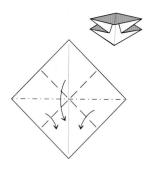

1 Start with a preliminary base.

2 Rotate the model by 180°.

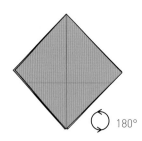

3 Fold the model in half lengthwise along both axes.

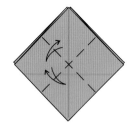

4 Fold the left corner in to touch the crease made previously. Unfold.

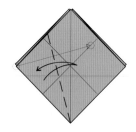

5 Fold the opposite edge and align the outer edge with the crease made previously.

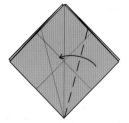

6 Fold the section up perpendicular to the model, separate the layers and squash flat.

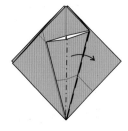

7 Fold the outer corners in to the middle of the upper section. Then unfold.

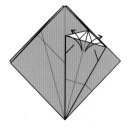

8 Fold down the edge causing the sides to fold in.

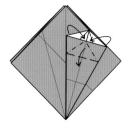

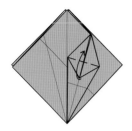

(9) Fold the lower triangle back up.

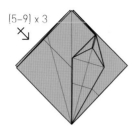

(10) Repeat steps 5 to 9 on the other side. Then behind.

(11) Fold the sides over front and back to expose the inside faces.

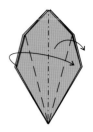

(12) Fold one side over and reverse out the inner section.

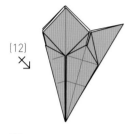

(13) Repeat step 12 on the other side.

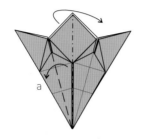

(14) Fold the model over at (a) to complete the process. Repeat behind.

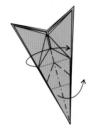

(15) Fold the model in half. At the same time reverse fold up the lower section.

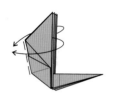

(16) Fold the outer petals over to the right, front and back.

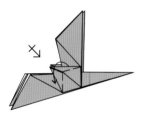

(17) Pinch and fold the middle section together. Repeat on the other three sections.

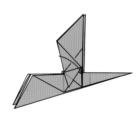

(18) Fold a petal over.

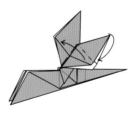

(19) Fold the section up again, separate the layers and squash flat.

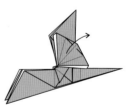

(20) Fold the petal out, causing the edges to fold in.

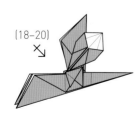

(21) Repeat steps 18 to 20 on the other three petals.

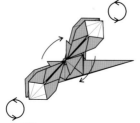

(22) Twist the petals and shape the flower.

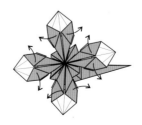

(23) Open up the petals.

(24) Complete.

Four-petal Balloon Flower *

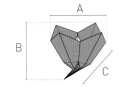

A	6.5cm	(2½in)
B	6cm	(2⅓in)
C	6.5cm	(2½in)

18 X 18CM (7 X 7IN)

START WITH A SQUARE, COLOURED SIDE UP.

Start with a frog base,
(Step 9 of the Classic Lily
pages 64-66).

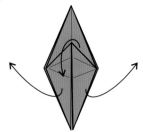

1 Open the model out to a square.

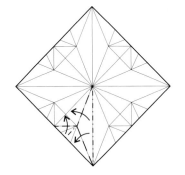

2 White side up, pinch the point together and fold it over to the left.

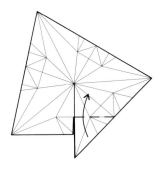

3 Fold the lower point up.

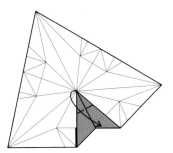

4 Fold the corner back out again.

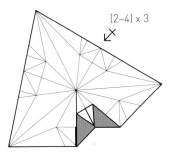

(2-4) x 3

5 Repeat steps 2-4 on the other three corners.

6 Pinch the base of the flower and bend it to the left.

7 Complete.

Pentagon

A pentagon can be used to make flowers with five petals. The following process shows how a regular pentagon can be made from a square.

18 X 18CM (7 X 7IN)

A   16.75cm   (2½in)
B   17.5cm   (2½in)

START WITH A SQUARE, COLOURED SIDE DOWN.

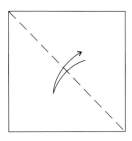

1 Fold and unfold the square in half diagonally.

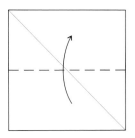

2 Fold the lower half of the square up along the middle.

3 Fold one corner in to the lower edge, and unfold.

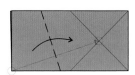

4 Fold the lower left corner in to touch the point where the creases cross.

5 Fold that corner back to the left to align the edges.

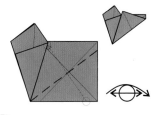

6 Fold the lower right corner up to align the lower edge with the adjacent folded edge. Then turn the model over left to right.

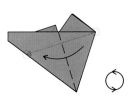

7 Fold in the model in half by folding the outer edges together and rotate slightly.

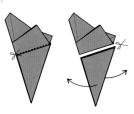

8 Cut through the layers along the edge. Separate the sections. Unfold lower part.

9 Pentagon complete.

Five-petal Blossom Flower ✳

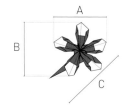

A	6.5cm	(2½in)
B	6.5cm	(2½in)
C	6cm	(2⅓in)

x1

18 X 18CM (7 X 7IN)

START WITH A PENTAGON (SEE PAGE 43), COLOURED SIDE DOWN.

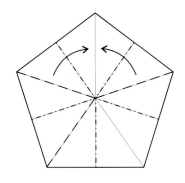

(1) Fold the sides in from the middle to bring all of the corners together.

(2) Fold the sides of the upper layer in to overlap each other. These folds should be a third of the way in.

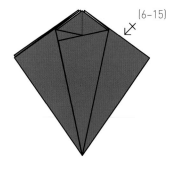

(6–15)

(3) Repeat steps 6 to 15 of the four-petal blossom flower (see page 40).

(4) Fold the outer sides up to open out the flower head.

(5) Pinch the triangular sections together and tease out the petals.

(6) Open out the petals.

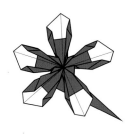

(7) Complete.

Five-petal Balloon Flower ✳✳

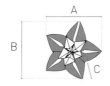

x1

A 6.5cm (2½in)
B 6.5cm (2½in)
C 6cm (2⅓in)

18 X 18CM (7 X 7IN)

START WITH A PENTAGON, COLOURED SIDE DOWN (SEE PAGE 43).

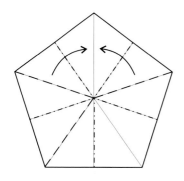

1 Fold the sides in from the middle to bring all of the corners together.

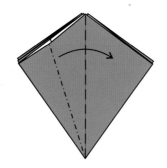

2 Fold the sides in, separate the layers and squash flat. Repeat on all sides.

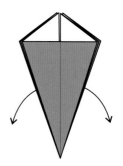

3 Open out to a pentagon.

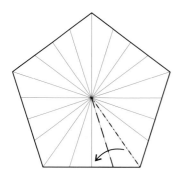

4 Repeat steps 2 to 4 of the forget-me-not on each side.

5 Rotate the model. The next step will show a side view of the model.

6 Pinch the base of the flower.

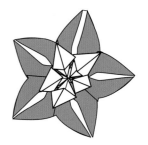

7 Complete.

Palm Leaf

*

The palm leaf is based on a pleated folded texture that forms the leaf pattern. It looks interesting because the stalk and leaf have different textures according to how the paper is folded. Experiment with the model by making it with different patterned papers.

18 X 18CM (7 X 7IN)

x1

A 6.5cm (2½in)
B 18cm   (7in)
C 2.5cm (1in)

START WITH A SQUARE, COLOURED SIDE UP.

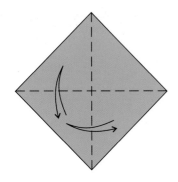

(1) Fold and unfold the square in half diagonally along both axes.

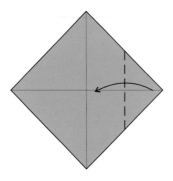

(2) Fold the right corner in to the middle.

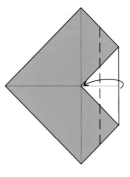

(3) Fold the right edge in to the middle.

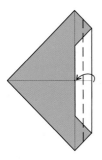

(4) Fold the same edge into the middle crease again.

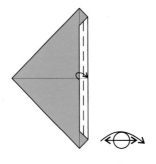

(5) Fold both layers of the edge over then turn the model over.

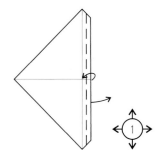

(6) Fold the outer edge in, then unfold back to a square.

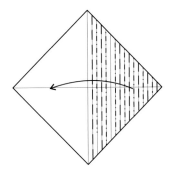

(7) Fold the right side up along the creased made previously, pleating the section to the crease adjacent to the middle.

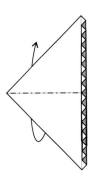

(8) Fold the lower section to the back along the middle crease.

(9) Fold the corner over diagonally, starting the crease at the upper corner.

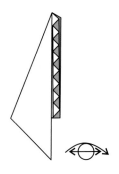

(10) Turn the model over left to right.

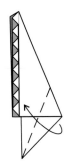

(11) Fold the lower right corner in diagonally.

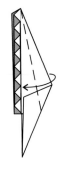

(12) Fold the upper right edge in.

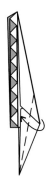

(13) Fold the lower edge in again.

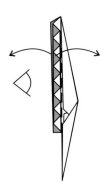

(14) Open out the fan section.

(15) Complete.

Cactus in a Pot

**

The cactus is a slightly more advanced project. It slots neatly into its pot and is designed to be displayed in the home or on a desk. Unlike the conventional cactus, this one requires no watering at all.

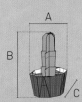

x3

18 X 18CM (7 X 7IN)

A 8.5cm (3⅓in)
B 15.5cm (6in)
C 8.5cm (3⅓in)

CACTUS

START WITH A SQUARE, COLOURED SIDE UP.

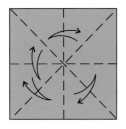

(1) Fold and unfold the square in half lengthwise and diagonally. Then turn the paper over left to right.

(2) Fold the lower right corner up to touch the vertical middle crease. The fold starts from the lower left corner.

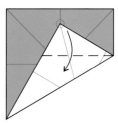

(3) Fold the edge back down to the lower folded edge.

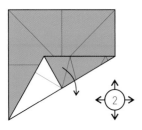

(4) Unfold the model back to a square (step 2).

(5) Fold the left edge in to the diagonal crease made in step 2 .

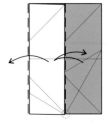

(6) Fold and unfold the right edge aligned with the crease. Unfold back to a square.

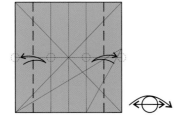

(7) Fold and unfold the sides between the creases made previously. Then turn the model over left to right.

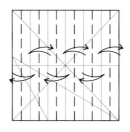

(8) Fold and unfold between all the vertical creases made previously.

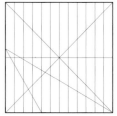

(9) Turn the model over left to right.

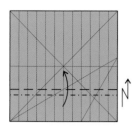

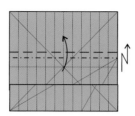

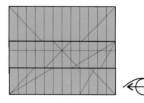

10 Fold the lower section up and down again, to form a pleat in the middle.

11 Fold the upper section up and down again, to form a pleat.

12 Turn the model over left to right.

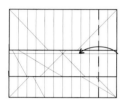

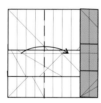

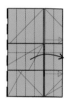

13 Fold the right section in along the second crease.

14 Fold the left side in to touch the opposite folded edge.

15 Tuck the right side into the left.

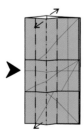

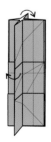

16 This shows the fold in progress. Note the left side will fold over the right side.

17 Push the right side in and pinch the adjacent creases together to start to shape the plant.

18 Fold the folded sections to be flat against the model.

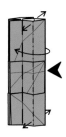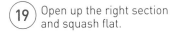

19 Open up the right section and squash flat.

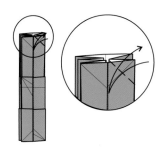

20 Fold in the upper right corner, and unfold.

21 Reverse fold the corner into the model.

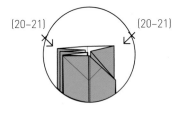

(20–21) (20–21)

22 Repeat steps 20 to 21 on the other three corners.

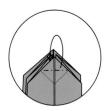

23 Fold the corners behind.

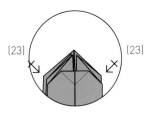

[23] [23]

24 Repeat step 23 on the other three corners.

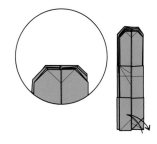

25 Upper section complete. Then fold and unfold the lower right corner.

26 Fold the lower edge up, causing the paper in the layer beneath to open out. Squash this flat.

27 Fold the edge back again.

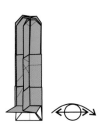

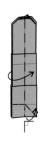

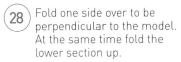

(28) Fold one side over to be perpendicular to the model. At the same time fold the lower section up.

(29) Turn the model over left to right.

(30) Repeat step 28 and fold the edge out to be perpendicular to the model.

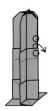

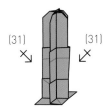

(31) X   (31) X

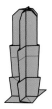

(31) Hold the lower section and slide it out slightly to shape the plant.

(32) Repeat the process on the pleats to shape the cactus.

(33) Complete.

TO ASSEMBLE

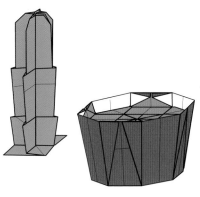

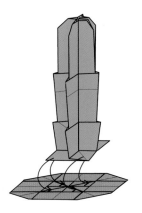

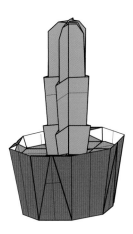

(34) Now insert the cactus into the pot. For pot instructions see pages 29-31.

(35) Insert the edges into the cross-shaped space. The flat base should fit inside the middle folded section.

(36) Complete.

Pine Tree

***

The pine tree is a more complex project that evolved from creating a texture
from sink folds. The sink fold is one of the most complex origami processes,
but the folding sequence shown here simplifies it.

18 X 18CM (7 X 7IN)   x1

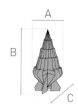

A 3.5cm   (1⅓in)
B 6cm   (2⅓in)
C 3.5cm   (1⅓in)

START WITH A SQUARE, COLOURED SIDE UP.

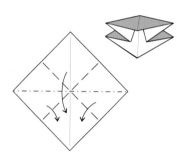

1 Fold the upper point down and fold the outer corners in to make a preliminary base.

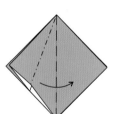

2 Fold the corner up, separate the layers and squash down flat.

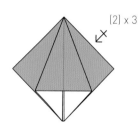

(2) x 3

3 Repeat step 2 on the other three corners.

4 Fold up the left corner and squash flat.

5 Fold the edge back to the left.

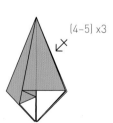

(4–5) x3

6 Repeat steps 4 to 5 on the other three corners.

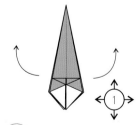

7 Unfold back to a square.

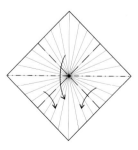

8 Fold the upper section down and fold the outer corners in along creases made previously to make a preliminary base.

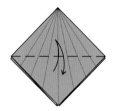   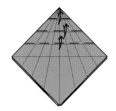

⑨ Fold the lower section up along the middle crease, and unfold.

⑩ Fold the upper corner to the middle crease, and unfold.

⑪ Fold and unfold, dividing the upper section into four.

⑫ Make new creases by folding and unfolding creases made previously.

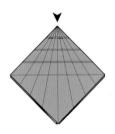 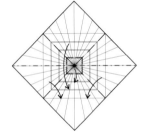  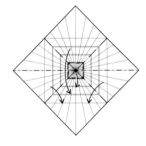

⑬ Sink fold the upper corner into the model.

⑭ Step 13 can be made by opening up to a square, then folding the point inside.

⑮ Reverse fold the inner corner up again.

⑯ Step 15 can be achieved by opening up to a square and folding the inner section in and out again.

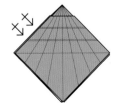 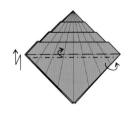 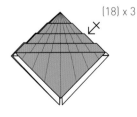 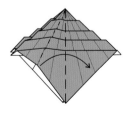

⑰ Repeat the double sink process on the other two creases below the centre point.

⑱ Fold the lower edge up and down again to form a narrow pleat at the lowest crease.

⑲ Repeat step 18 on the other three sides of the model.

(18) x 3

⑳ Fold the left corner up, separate the layers and open out the paper.

(21) Push the upper section in and open out the paper below and squash it flat.

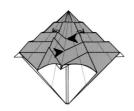

(22) Continue folding the sides apart and squashing the paper.

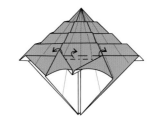

(23) Fold the lower section up and down again to form a pleat.

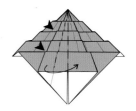

(24) Fold the point up to be perpendicular to the model, separate the layers and squash flat.

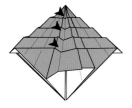

(25) Push in the raised sections and flatten.

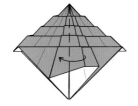

(26) Fold the edge back over.

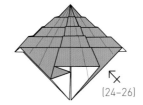

(27) Repeat steps 24 to 26 on the other side.

(24–26)

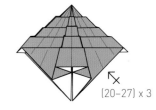

(28) Repeat steps 20 to 27 on the other three faces.

(20–27) x 3

(29) Fold the right side over to the left.

(30) Fold the lower edge up, and at the same time fold the right diagonal edge in.

(31) Fold the corner back down.

(32) Fold the corner behind and into the model.

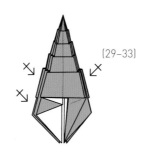

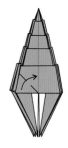

(29–33)

(33) Fold the left side back over to the right.

(34) Repeat steps 29 to 33 on the other corners.

(35) Fold the right side over.

(36) Fold the left corner up.

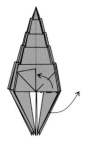

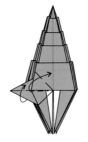
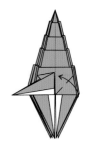

(37) Fold the right corner up and squash the point.

(38) Fold the right side over. to the left.

(39) Fold the lower corner back up.

(40) Fold the right corner up.

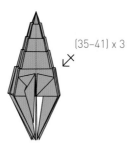
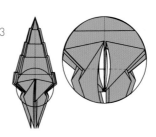
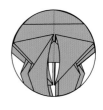

(35–41) x 3

(41) Turn the left point inside out to make it point downwards.

(42) Repeat step 35 to 41 on the other three corners.

(43) Fold the inner corner up.

(44) Detail complete.

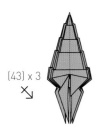

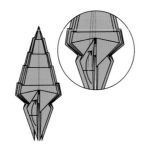

(43) x 3

45 Repeat step 43 on the other three sides.

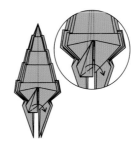

46 Fold the point up.

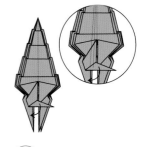

47 Then down again.

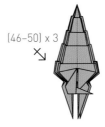

48 Then unfold the point.

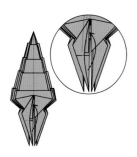

49 Reverse fold the corner into the point.

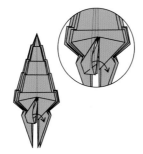

50 Fold the corner back down again.

(46–50) x 3

51 Repeat steps 46 to 50 on the other three sides.

52 Fold the point over.

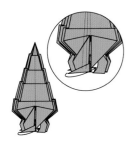

53 Fold the corner back and tuck it into the adjacent pocket.

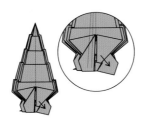

54 Fold the corner over the folded point.

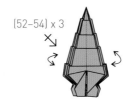

(52–54) x 3

55 Repeat steps 52 to 54 on the other three sides open out the layers.

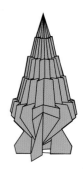

56 Complete

FLOWERS

Classic Lily & Iris

*

The classic lily is a traditional design based on a frog base. The four corners of the square become the petals of the flower. The lily is also the basis for the stem of the rose (see page 72) and the four-petal balloon flower (see page 42).

18 X 18CM (7 X 7IN)

A 13.5cm   (5⅓in)
B 6.75cm   (2½in)
C 13.5cm   (5⅓in)

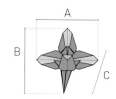

A 11cm   (4⅓in)
B 7.5cm   (3in)
C 3.5cm   (1⅓in)

LILY

START WITH A SQUARE, COLOURED SIDE UP.

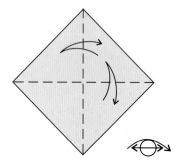

(1) Fold and unfold the square in half diagonally then turn the paper over left to right.

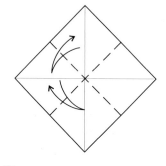

(2) Fold and unfold along the paper lengthwise.

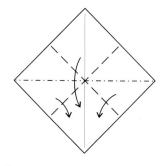

(3) Fold the upper section down and fold the outer corners in to refold the creases made previously.

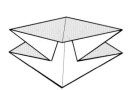

(4) Fold in progress.

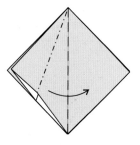

(5) Fold the corner up, separate the layers and squash flat.

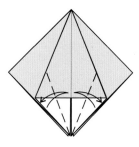

(6) Fold and unfold the outer edges in to the middle crease.

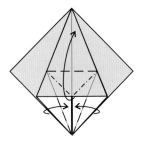

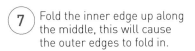

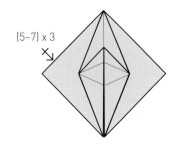

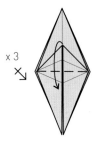

(5–7) x 3

x 3

7 Fold the inner edge up along the middle, this will cause the outer edges to fold in.

8 Repeat steps 5 to 7 on the other three faces.

9 Fold the corners of the middle section down. Repeat on the three other faces.

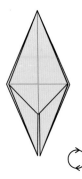

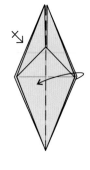

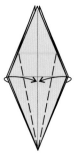

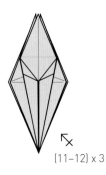

○ 180°

(11–12) x 3

10 Rotate the model by 180°.

11 Fold one side over to expose the adjacent face, front and back.

12 Fold the outer corner edges to the middle.

13 Repeat steps 11 to 12 on the other three faces.

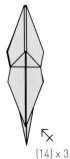

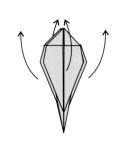

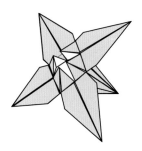

(14) x 3

14 Fold the upper point down.

15 Repeat step 14 on the other three faces.

16 Fold the outer petals up and open the flower.

17 Complete.

IRIS

START WITH STEP 8 OF THE LILY.

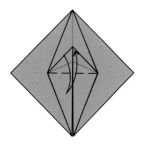

① Fold the corner of the middle section up and down.

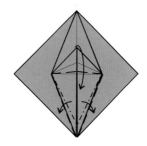

② Open the lower section to expose the underside of the paper. At the same time fold the upper corner down.

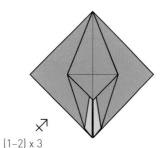

(1–2) x 3

③ Repeat steps 1 to 2 on the other three faces.

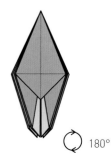

180°

④ Rotate the model by 180°.

⑤ Fold the right side over to expose the adjacent face.

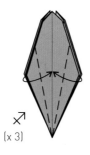

(x 3)

⑥ Fold the outer corners in to the middle. Repeat the process on the other three faces.

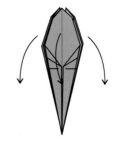

⑦ Fold the front section down, then fold and flatten the petals.

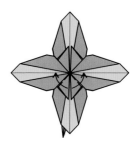

⑧ Fold the inner corners up.

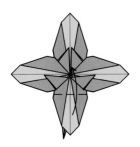

⑨ Fold the lower section up.

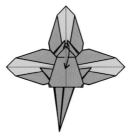

⑩ Fold the tip over.

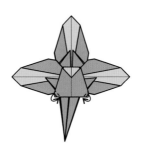

⑪ Fold the lower corners behind.

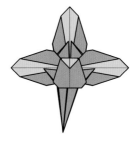

⑫ Complete.

Calla Lily

**

The calla or arum lily comes in various colours including white, purple, yellow and orange. It has many associations, from purity and resurrection in religious art to holiness, faith and purity. When the flower blooms in spring, it is also a symbol of youth.

18 X 18CM (7 X 7IN)   x1

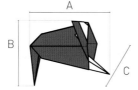

A 12.5cm   (5in)
B 7cm   (2¾in)
C 5cm   (2in)

START WITH A SQUARE, COLOURED SIDE UP.

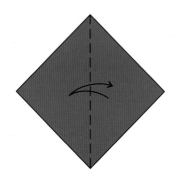

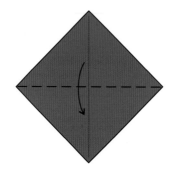

1. Fold and unfold the square in half diagonally.

2. Fold the upper section down along the middle.

3. Fold and unfold the outer corner in to the middle crease.

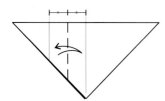

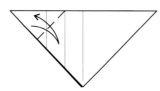

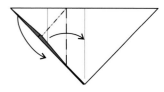

4. Fold and unfold between the creases.

5. Fold and unfold the corner down to make the upper edge touch the crease made in step 4.

6. Fold the corner up to be perpendicular to the model, separate the layers and squash flat.

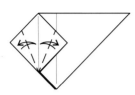

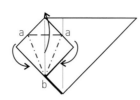

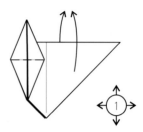

7 Fold and unfold the outer edges in to the middle crease.

8 Fold up the upper layer, this will cause the outer edges to fold in.

9 Open out the model back to a square.

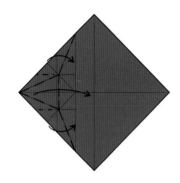

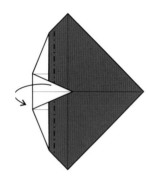

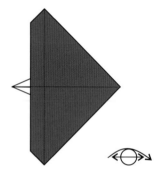

10 Fold the left corner in to the model, using the creases made previously.

11 Fold the outer section behind the model.

12 Turn the model over left to right.

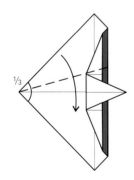

13 Fold the upper section down This is about a third of the model.

14 Fold the lower section up over the folded edge.

15 Fold the upper right edge over along the edge of the layer beneath.

(16) Fold the lower right edge over the folded edge.

(17) Fold the right corner over.

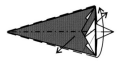

(18) Separate the layers and squash model flat. The next step shows the side view.

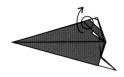

(19) Hold the upper section and slide it up.

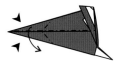

(20) Pinch the end of the flower and fold it down.

(21) Flower head complete.

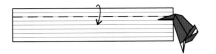

(22) To add a stem: Place the base of the flower head onto a paper rectangle of green paper and fold the upper edge of paper over it (see page 90 Stem assembly, steps 1-6).

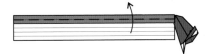

(23) Fold the lower edge up and wrap it around the upper folded edge.

(24) Pinch the stem together and shape the stalk.

(25) Complete.

(26) Make several flowers to form a bunch.

Rose

**

The rose is one of the most iconic flowers. Depending on its colour, its associations include red for romance, white for innocence and yellow for friendship. Pink is often linked to gratitude.

18 X 18CM (7 X 7IN)

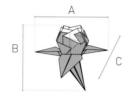

A 10cm (4in)
B 10cm (4in)
C 10cm (4in)

START WITH A SQUARE, COLOURED SIDE UP.

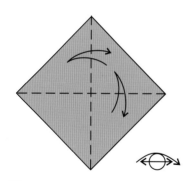

1. Fold and unfold the square in half diagonally. Then turn the paper over left to right.

2. Fold and unfold along the middle of the paper lengthwise.

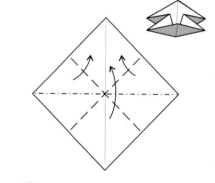

3. Fold the lower section up and fold the outer corners in to make a preliminary base.

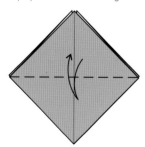

4. Fold and unfold the upper layer along the middle.

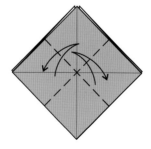

5. Fold and unfold the model in half lengthwise along both axes.

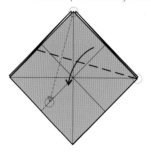

6. Fold the upper corner of the upper layer down to touch the crease folded previously.

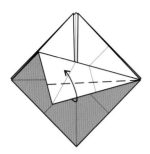

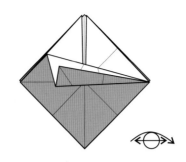

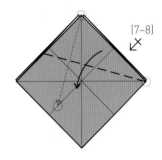

(7–8)

7 Fold the lower layer up again.

8 Turn the model over left to right.

9 Repeat steps 7 to 8.

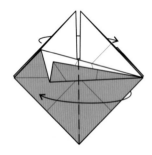

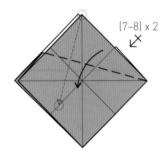

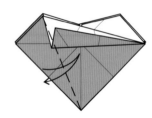

(7–8) x 2

10 Fold the front and rear sides over to expose the other faces.

11 Repeat steps 7 to 8 on the front and reverse.

12 Fold the left side in to the middle crease and unfold.

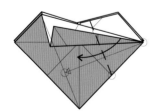

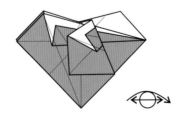

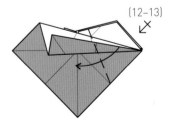

(12–13)

13 Fold the right side in so that the outer corner touches the crease made in step 12.

14 Turn the model over left to right.

15 Repeat steps 12 to 13.

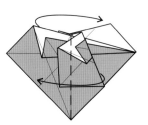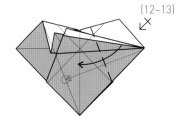

16 Fold the front and back sections over to expose the hidden faces.

17 Repeat steps 12 to 13.

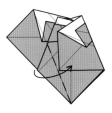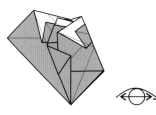

18 Fold the lower edge in along the folds made previously.

19 Turn the model over left to right.

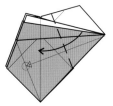

20 Repeat steps 17 to 18.

21 Fold the edges in on the hidden faces.

22 Rose head section complete.

ADDING A LEAF TO THE ROSE HEAD

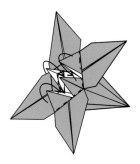

1. Make a lily (see pages 64-6), then fold in the corners of the middle section.

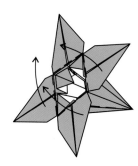

2. Fold up the outer leaves and flatten the model.

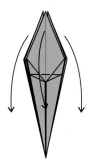

3. Fold the outer leaves down.

4. Insert the rose-head section into the leaf section. Ensure that the ridges in the petal section fit into the spaces in the leaf section.

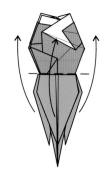

5. Fold the leaves back up.

6. Fold the lower section up to lock the petal and leaf section together. Pinch the stalk together.

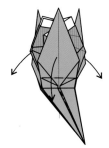

7. Fold the leaves back down again.

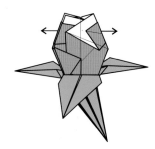

8. Open out the flower section.

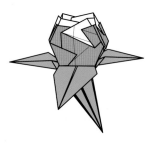

9. Complete.

Tulip

**

The tulip is a two-piece model that uses the corners of the square
to make the flower petals.

18 X 18CM (7 X 7IN)

x1

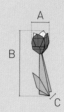

A 4cm   (1½in)
B 21cm   (8¼in)
C 6.8cm (2½in)

FOR THE TULIP HEAD, START WITH A SQUARE, COLOURED SIDE UP,
AND FOLLOW STEPS 1 TO 11 OF NUTS IN A BOWL (SEE PAGES 18-20).

1 Rotate the model by 180°.

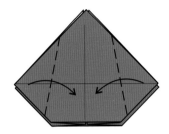

2 Fold the outer corners of the upper layer to a point approximately midway between the horizontal crease and the lower edge.

3 Fold the lower corner in.

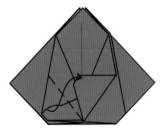

4 Fold the opposite corner in and tuck the opposite corner beneath the folded edge.

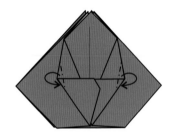

5 Fold the outer corners of this section behind on both sides.

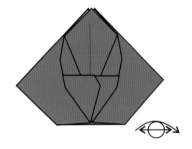

6 Turn the model over left to right.

[2–5]

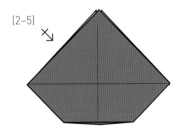

7 Repeat steps 2 to 5.

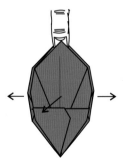

8 Insert a finger and open out the flower head.

9 Shape the tips of the upper petals.

FOR THE STEM, START WITH A GREEN SQUARE THE SAME SIZE AS THE ROSE HEAD, COLOURED SIDE DOWN.

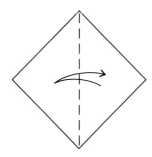

1. Fold and unfold the square in half diagonally.

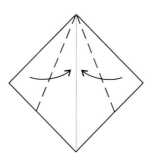

2. Fold the corners in to the middle crease, starting the folds at the upper corner.

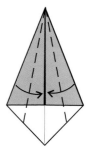

3. Fold the outer edges in again.

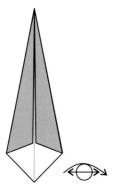

4. Turn the model over left to right.

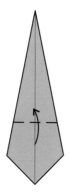

5. Fold the lower section up.

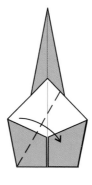

6. Fold the left side over as shown.

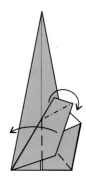

7. Fold the section back over.

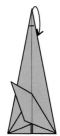

8. Fold the tip of the model over.

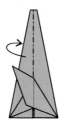

9. Fold the reverse sides of the model together.

10. Insert the stalk into the base of the flower head.

11. Complete.

Water Lily
**

The water lily is based on a blintz frog base that produces an eight-pointed base.
Petals are built up around the centre of the square and ultimately the model unfolds
or 'blooms' around the inner section.

18 X 18CM (7 X 7IN)

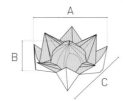

A 7.5cm   (3in)
B 3.5cm   (1⅓in)
C 7.5cm   (3in)

START WITH A SQUARE, COLOURED SIDE UP.

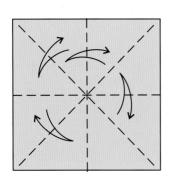

(1) Fold and unfold the square
in half lengthwise and
diagonally along all axes.

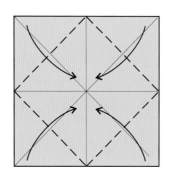

(2) Fold the corners in to
the middle.

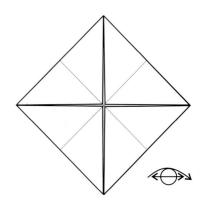

(3) Turn the model over left
to right.

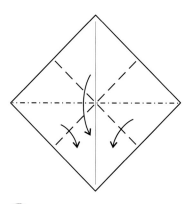

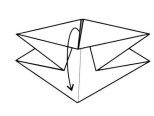

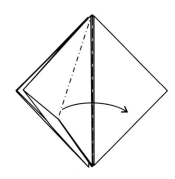

4 Fold the upper corner down and fold the sides in, making a preliminary base.

5 Fold in progress.

6 Fold the left corner of the upper layer up, separate the layers and squash the section flat.

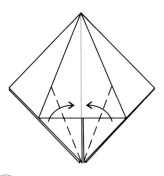

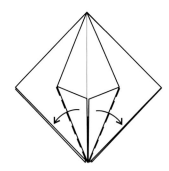

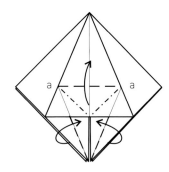

7 Fold the corners of this section in to the middle.

8 Then unfold.

9 Fold the edge up along the middle (a–a). This will cause the lower edges to fold in.

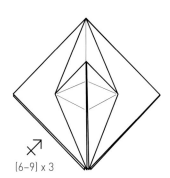

(6–9) x 3

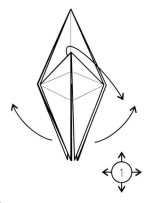

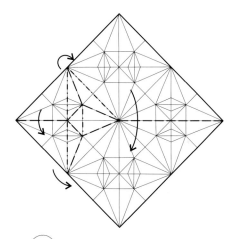

10 Repeat steps 6 to 9 on the other three faces.

11 Unfold the model back to a square.

12 Fold the square in half and re-fold the outer section.

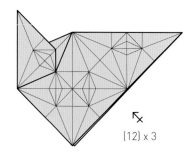

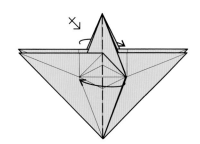

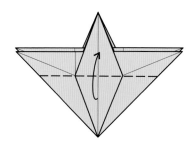

(13) Refold the creases on the other three corners.

(14) Fold the front and back sections over to expose the hidden faces Repeat behind.

(15) Fold the lower corner up.

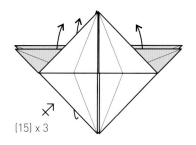

(16) Fold the corners up on the other three sides.

(17) Fold the left corner in and out again.

(18) Refold the corner and turn it inside out.

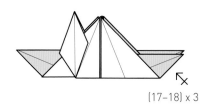

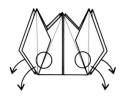

(19) Repeat steps 17 to 18 on the other three corners.

(20) Hold the model where indicated and open out the middle section.

(21) Complete.

Fuchsia
**

The fuchsia is shaped differently to other flower as it hangs downwards. This model uses a base called a blintz frog base to create the inner and outer petals. The same base is used for the water lily on page 80.

18 X 18CM (7 X 7IN)

x1

A
B
C

A 9cm (3½in)
B 8.5cm (3⅓in)
C 9cm (3½in)

START WITH STEP 14 OF THE WATER LILY (PAGES 80-3).

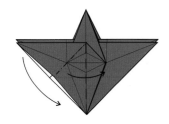

1. Fold the left corner of the upper layer up, separate the layers and squash flat.

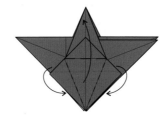

2. Fold the lower section up and fold in the sides.

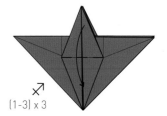

(1-3) x 3

3. Fold the upper corner back down again. Repeat steps 1 to 3 on the other three sides.

4. Fold over one side on the front and reverse.

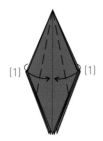

(1)   (1)

5. Fold the upper layer of the outer edges in to the middle crease.

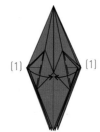

(1)   (1)

6. Fold over the next layer on both sides.

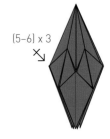

(5–6) x 3

7. Repeat steps 5 to 6 on the other three sides.

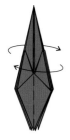

8. Fold over sides front and behind.

9. Fold the lower corners up on all four sides.

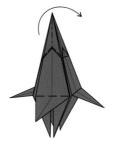

10. Pinch the top of the model and fold the tip over.

11. Flower head complete. The flower heads can be added to a plant.

Bunch of Flowers

✶✶

This series of eight-petalled flowers can be made into a bouquet. Try combining flowers of complementary colours or add alternative flowers on stems. An origami bouquet is a great way to celebrate a first (paper) wedding anniversary or a birthday.

18 X 18CM (7 X 7IN)

x1

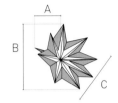

A 9cm	(3½in)
B 9cm	(3½in)
C 6cm	(2⅓in)

START WITH A SQUARE, COLOURED SIDE DOWN.

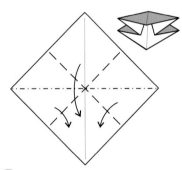

(1) Fold the upper section down and fold in the sides to make a preliminary base.

(2) Fold the corner up, separate the layers and squash flat.

(3) Fold the left side over to the right.

(2–3) x 3

(4) Repeat steps 2 to 3 on the other three corners.

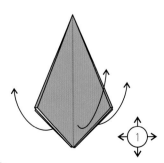

(5) Open the model back to a square.

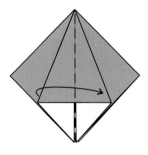

(6) Fold the corners in to the middle.

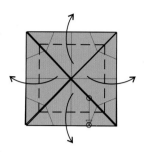

(7) Fold the corners out so that the edges of the corner touch the crease on the folded edge.

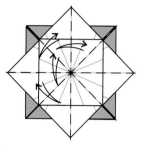

(8) Refold the creases made previously and unfold.

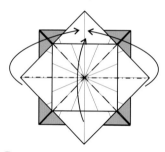

(9) Fold the lower section up and fold up the corners.

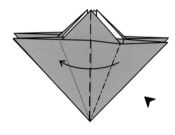

(10) Fold the corner over, open and squash flat.

(10)

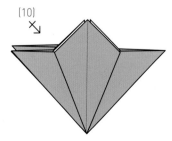

(11) Repeat step 10 on the other three sides.

(12) Fold the upper edges in to the middle crease, and unfold.

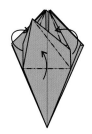

13 Fold the upper section down and back again and reverse fold the sides into the model.

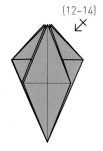

14 Fold in progress.

(12–14)

15 Repeat steps 12 to 14 on the other faces.

(16) x 3

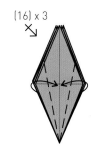

16 Fold the edges in to the middle on all four faces.

17 Fold the lower point up.

18 Pinch the stalk together and start to unfold the petals.

19 Unfold the petals to open the flower.

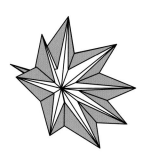

20 Complete.

VARIATION 1

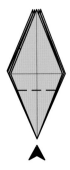 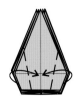 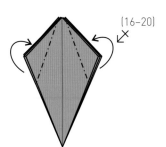 

(1) Start at step 16 of the flower on page 59, coloured side down, Fold the stalk in half.

(2) Fold the edges in on all of the faces, then open out the flower.

(3) Complete.

VARIATION 2

(1) At step 12, fold the edges in, but add some more shape at the top of the petals.

(2) Reverse fold the edges inside and complete the flower by following steps 16 to 20.

(16–20)

(3) Complete.

FOR THE FLOWER STEM, START WITH A RECTANGLE, COLOURED SIDE DOWN.

18 cm (7in)

6 cm (2⅓in)

30cm (12in)

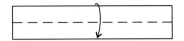  

(1) Fold the rectangle in half.

(2) Then fold it in half again.

(3) Then in half again.

4 Unfold.

5 Turn the paper over.

6 Insert the flower at one end of the rectangle and start to roll the stalk around it.

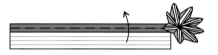

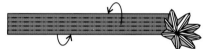

7 Roll the stalk around the flower.

8 Continue rolling the stalk.

9 Pinch the stalk and fold the rolled stalk in half.

10 Now make a collection of flowers on stems.

SECURING THE BOUQUET

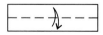

1 Fold the rectangle along the middle and unfold.

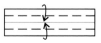

2 Fold the edges to the middle.

3 Wrap the band around the flowers and secure. Trim the ends of the stems.

FRUIT AND VEGETABLES

Strawberry

**

This project is made from double-sided paper, with the leaves appearing on the reverse side. The final model is a closed space that is inflated to form the fruit.

18 X 18CM (7 X 7IN)

x1

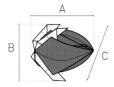

A 6cm   (2⅓in)
B 6cm   (2⅓in)
C 6cm   (2⅓in)

x1

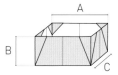

A 9cm   (3½in)
B 4.5cm   (1¾in)
C 9cm   (3½in)

START WITH A SQUARE, COLOURED SIDE DOWN.

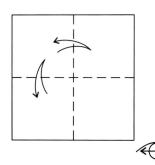

(1) Fold and unfold the square in half lengthwise along both axes. Then turn the paper over, left to right.

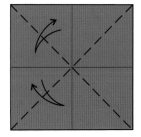

(2) Fold and unfold the square diagonally along the middle.

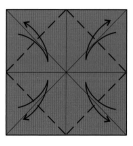

(3) Fold the outer corners in to touch the middle, then unfold.

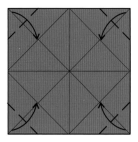

(4) Fold the corners in to touch the points where the creases made previously touch.

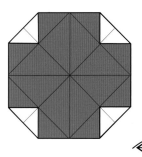

(5) Turn the model over left to right.

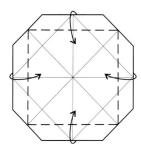

(6) Fold the outer edges in on all sides.

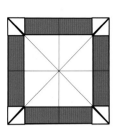

 45°

7 Rotate the model 45° anticlockwise.

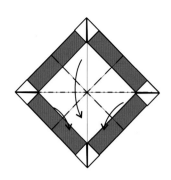

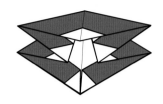

8 Fold the outer corners in along the creases made previously to make a preliminary base shape.

9 Fold in progress.

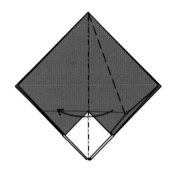

10 Fold one corner up, separate the layers and squash the point flat.

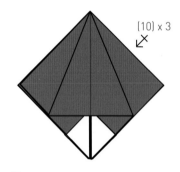

(10) x 3

11 Repeat step 10 on the other three sides.

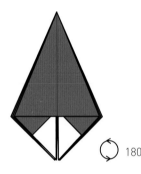

180°

12 Rotate the model 180° anticlockwise.

13 Fold one side over to the left.

14 Fold and unfold the upper corner.

15 Fold and unfold the upper layer to cause the upper point to touch the adjacent corners.

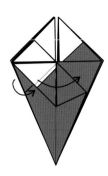

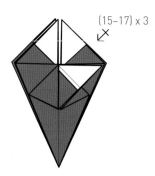

(15–17) x 3

16 Fold one side over along the crease made previously.

17 Fold the point over to the right and refold the crease made in step 15.

18 Repeat steps 15 to 17 on the other three points.

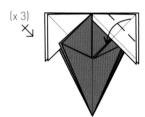

(x 3)

19 Fold out the paper from inside the folded corners. As a variation the leaves can be left as they are.

20 Fold in the corner to shape the leaf. Repeat this on the other three corners.

21 Fold over one side on the front and behind to expose the unfolded sides.

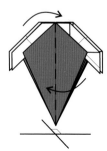

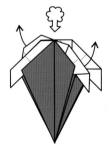

22 Pinch two layers together and fold the front and back sections over to be perpendicular to the middle.

23 Pinch the front and rear edges together, fold them out and up to open out and shape the lower fruit.

24 Complete.

MAKING THE PUNNET
START WITH A SQUARE, COLOURED SIDE UP.

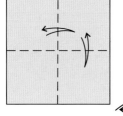

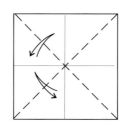

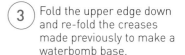

In progress.

(1) Fold and unfold the square in half lengthwise along both axes. Then turn the paper over left to right.

(2) Fold and unfold the square diagonally.

(3) Fold the upper edge down and re-fold the creases made previously to make a waterbomb base.

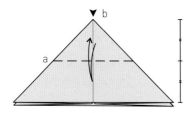

(4) Fold and unfold the outer corner (a) to the middle crease. Then sink the corner (b) inside the model.

(5) Rotate the model by 180°.

(6) Fold and unfold the corner in to the model.

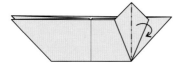

(6-8)

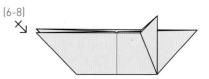

(7) Raise and squash the corner.

(8) Fold the edge behind.

(9) Repeat the corner-folding process (steps 6-8) on the other three corners.

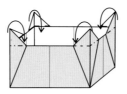

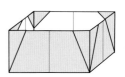

(10) Pull the sides apart, flatten the base and open the model.

(11) Fold the corners over the edge and into the model.

(12) Complete.

Mushroom

**

The Mushroom has a wide cap and a narrower stalk. It works best with patterned papers for the cap, so try experimenting with mottled and natural-looking patterns.

18 X 18CM (7 X 7IN)

x1

A 9.5cm (3¾in)
B 11.5cm (4½in)
C 3cm (1⅓in)

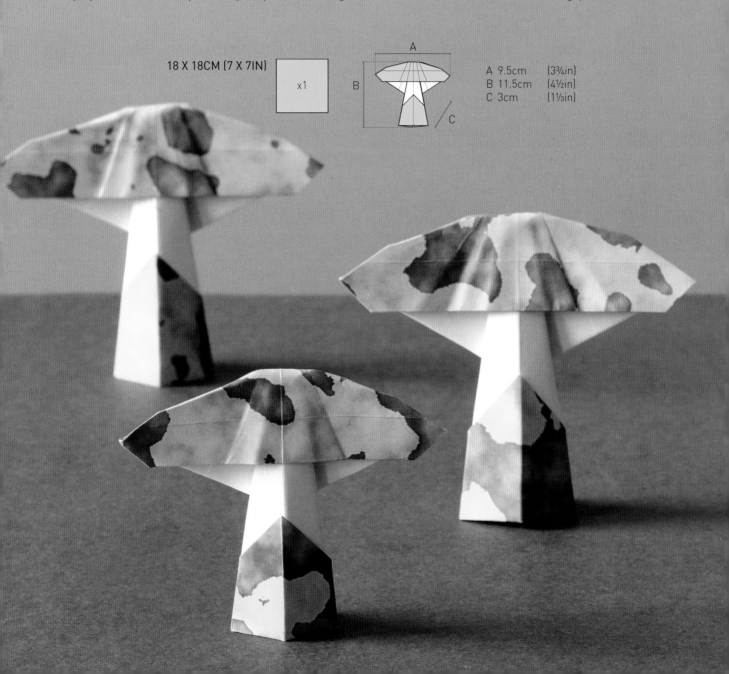

START WITH A SQUARE, COLOURED SIDE UP.

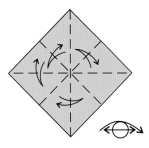

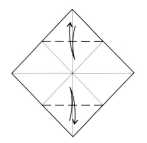

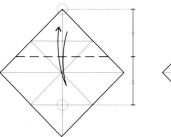

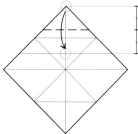

1. Fold and unfold the square in half lengthwise and diagonally along all axes. Then turn the paper over left to right.

2. Fold and unfold the upper and lower corners in to the middle.

3. Fold the upper corner down to the crease made previously in step 2 and unfold.

4. Fold the upper corner down to the crease made in step 3.

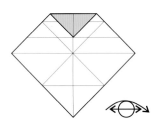

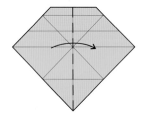

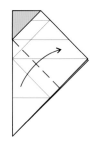

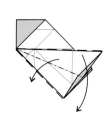

5. Turn the model over left to right.

6. Fold the model in half.

7. Fold the lower corner over.

8. Fold the corner up, separate the layers and squash flat.

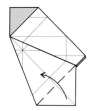

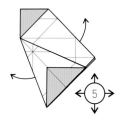

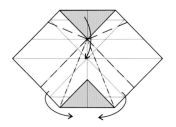

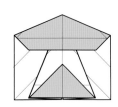

9. Fold the corner over.

10. Unfold to step 5, but leave the lower corner folded in.

11. Fold the outer sides in along the existing creases and fold the top section over.

12. Turn the model over left to right.

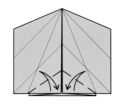

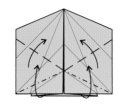

(13) Fold the upper layer in along the folded edges of the lower section. Then unfold.

(14) Fold the inner edges out to touch the creases made previously.

(15) Fold the edges up on both sides re folding the creases made in the previous steps.

(16) Fold one edge over to enable the outer edge to touch the middle.

(16–17)

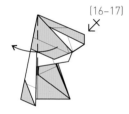

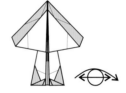

(17) Fold the upper layer back again. Then repeat steps 16 to 17 on the other side.

(18) Fold the lower corners up so they are aligned with the folded edge beneath.

(19) Turn the model over left to right.

(20) Fold out the trapped paper.

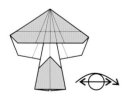

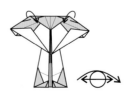

(21) Turn the model over left to right.

(22) Fold the corners in.

(23) Fold the corners in again to round the top. Then turn the model over.

(24) Complete.

Pear
**

The pear is constructed along the diagonal axis of the square and its shape is made by sliding the layers of the paper apart and together. Try making the model in yellows and greens as an alternative colourway.

18 X 18CM (7 X 7IN)   x1

A 9cm   (3½in)
B 15cm   (6in)
C 0.50cm (¼in)

START WITH A SQUARE, COLOURED SIDE DOWN.

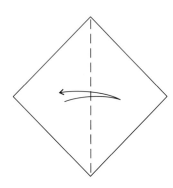

1 Fold and unfold the square in half diagonally.

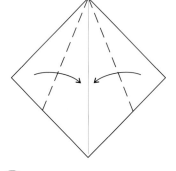

2 Fold the edges in to the middle crease.

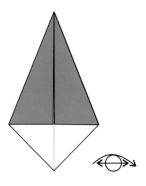

3 Turn the model over left to right.

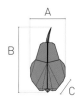

4 Fold the upper edge in to the middle crease.

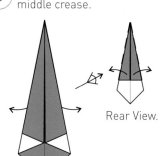

Rear View.

5 Fold the flaps out from behind to the front.

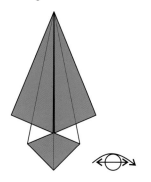

6 Turn the model over left to right.

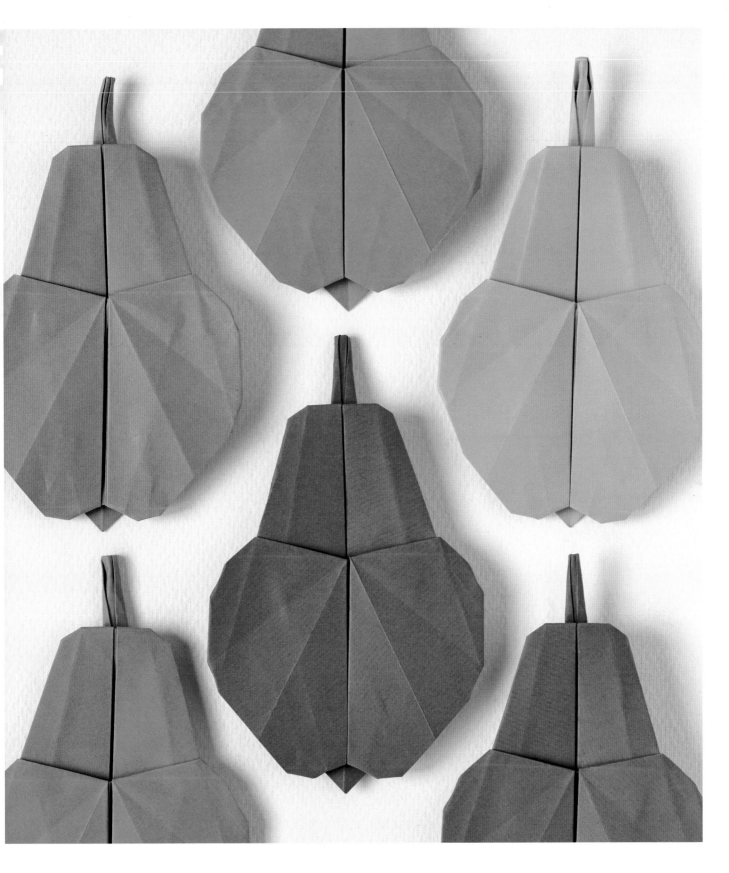

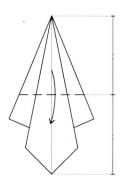
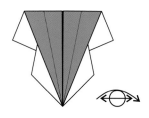

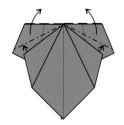

7. Fold the upper point down to touch the lower corner.

8. Turn the model over left to right.

9. Fold the corners out on both sides.

10. Fold the paper up where indicated and fold out the trapped paper.

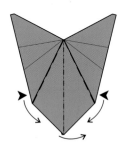

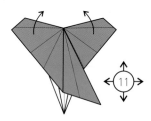
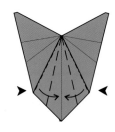

11. Push the sides together and fold the triangular section to the right over.

12. Fold the outer edge in to the adjacent crease and unfold.

13. Unfold the inner triangle. (Unfold to step 11.)

14. Fold the edges of the middle triangle in along the creases made previously.

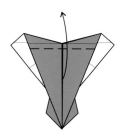
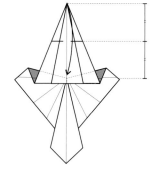
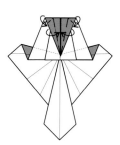

15. Turn the model over left to right.

16. Fold the point back up.

17. Fold the upper corner down to a point level with the folded edge beneath.

18. Fold the edges of the point in.

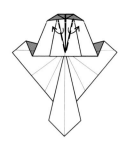

19 Unfold the previous step.

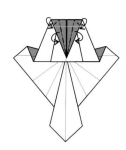

20 Fold the edges behind, along the creases made in the previous step.

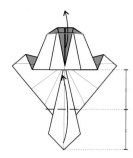

21 Fold the lower corner up to touch the folded edge above.

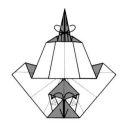

22 In the upper section fold in the edges. In the lower section fold the upper layers out to touch the adjacent edges.

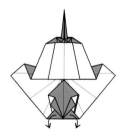

23 Fold the paper down where indicated and fold out the trapped paper.

24 Fold the corner of the lower section down.

25 Fold the edges of the lower section behind.

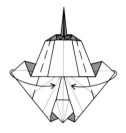

26 Fold the sides in.

27 Fold out the edges sideways.

28 Fold the corners in. Turn the model over left to right.

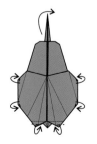

29 Fold all the corners in to shape the fruit.

30 Complete.

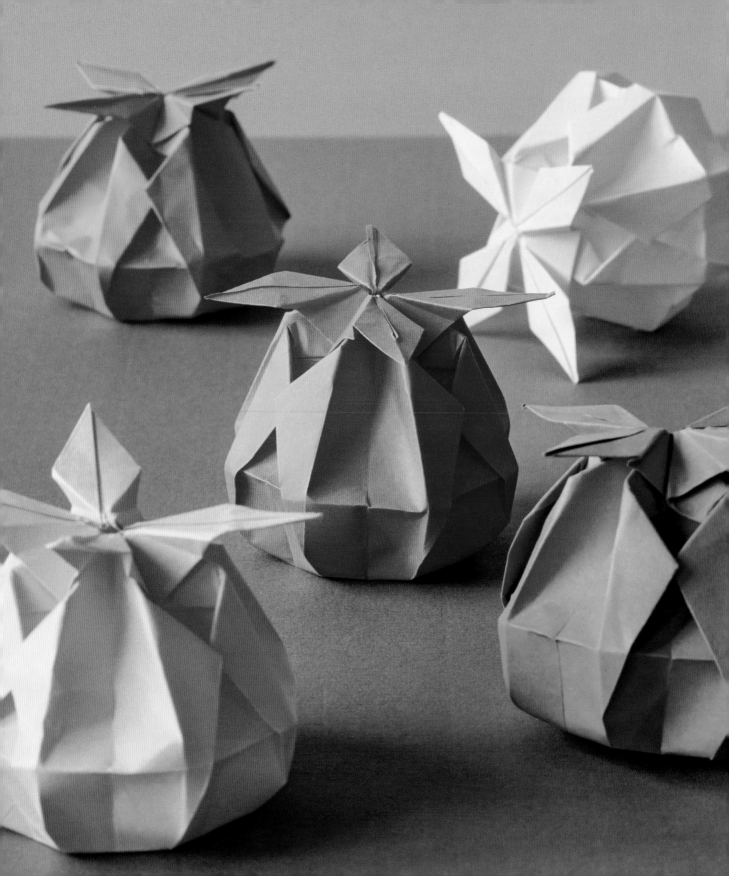

Tomato
**

The tomato is a three-dimensional model that inflates to make a juicy fruit. Similar to the strawberry, the leaves are made from the colour of the reverse of the square. Although most tomatoes are red, they also come in yellow, orange, green and black varieties.

18 X 18CM (7 X 7IN)   x1

A 6.75cm   (2½in)
B 6.75cm   (2½in)
C 5.50cm   (2in)

START WITH A SQUARE, COLOURED SIDE UP, AND FOLLOW STEPS 1 TO 5 OF THE NUTS IN A BOWL (SEE PAGE 18).

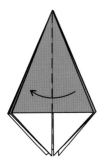

1 Start with step 6 of the nut (page 18). Fold the edge over front and back to expose the adjacent face.

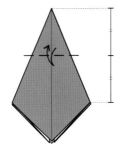

2 Fold and unfold the upper corner between the upper point and the folded edge of the paper in the layer beneath.

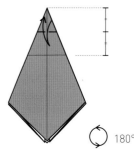
180°

3 Fold and unfold the flower corner to the crease made previously. Then Rotate the model by 180°.

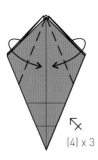

[4] x 3

4 Fold the upper corners in to the middle on all of the faces.

5 Fold the upper point down.

6 Fold the corners behind on both sides.

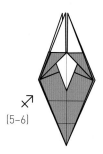

(5–6)

7 Repeat steps 5 to 6 on the other side.

8 Fold one side over and fold the corner to the right.

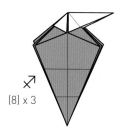

(8) x 3

9 Repeat step 8 on the other three faces.

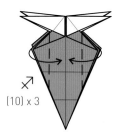

(10) x 3

10 Fold the corners in to the middle on all four faces.

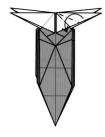

11 Fold the corner up, separate the layers and squash.

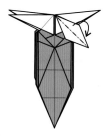

12 Fold the corner behind.

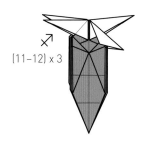

(11–12) x 3

13 Repeat Steps 11 to 12 on the other three leaves.

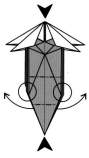

14 Hold the sides at the 'O's then open out and shape the model, reverse the lower point inside the model.

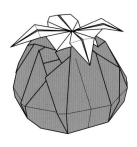

15 Complete.

Chilli Pepper
*

The chilli pepper is a simple model that fits neatly together in the final assembly
and uses the colours on both sides of the paper.

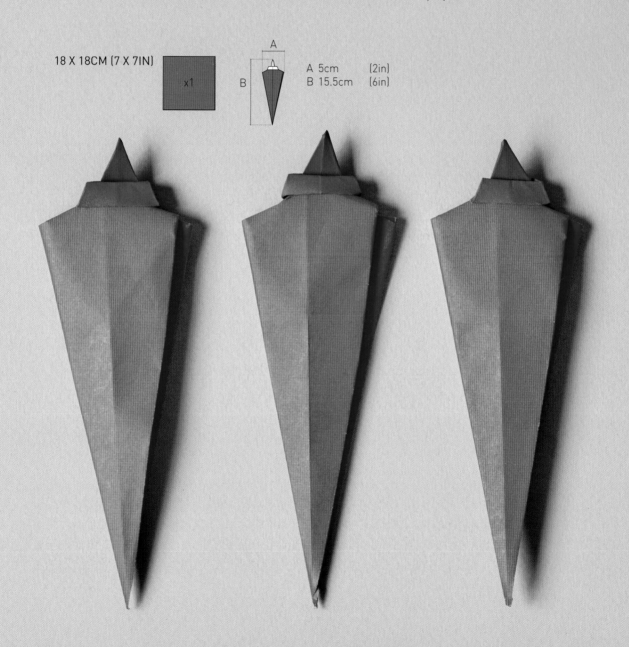

18 X 18CM (7 X 7IN)

x1

A
A
B

A 5cm (2in)
B 15.5cm (6in)

START WITH A SQUARE, COLOURED SIDE UP.

 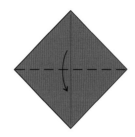 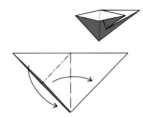 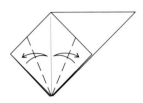

1. Fold and unfold the square in half diagonally. Then turn the paper over left to right.

2. Fold the upper section down along the middle.

3. Fold the point up to be perpendicular, then separate the layers and open and squash the point.

4. Fold the outer edges of the upper section in to the middle crease. Then unfold.

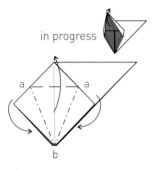 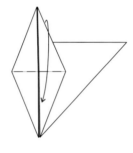 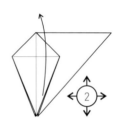 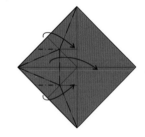

in progress

5. Fold the upper layer up along the line (a-a), this will cause the outer edges to fold in.

6. Fold the upper point back down.

7. Open up the model back to a square.

8. Fold the right section over and refold the creases made previously.

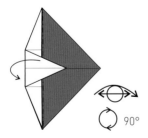   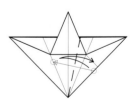

9. Fold the section behind. Then turn the model over and rotate by 90°.

10. Fold the outer edges of the model in to the middle.

11. Fold the sides back out again.

12. Fold the right edge in to the crease indicated and unfold.

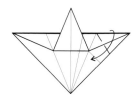

(13) Fold the outer corner in, adjacent to the diagonal crease.

(14) Fold the outer edge in to align with the adjacent crease.

(15) Fold edge in again.

(16) Fold the other side in to touch the adjacent crease. Then unfold.

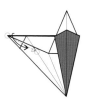

(17) Fold the outer corner in.

(18) Fold the outer edge in and then over again.

(19) Fold the corner behind to hold the two layers together.

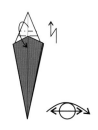

(20) Fold the upper point down over the adjacent corner then up again, making a zigzag fold. Turn the model over.

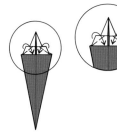

(21) Fold the corners of the upper section in.

(22) Fold the point down and up again making a zig-zag fold.

(23) Fold the outer edges in to shape the stalk.

(24) Complete

GARDEN LIFE

Butterfly

**

The butterfly emerges from a folded waterbomb base. Each of the corners folds out to become the tips of the wings. By experimenting with a variety of patterned papers you can really bring the butterfly to life.

18 X 18CM (7 X 7IN)   x1

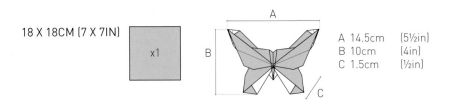

A 14.5cm (5½in)
B 10cm   (4in)
C 1.5cm   (½in)

START WITH A SQUARE, COLOURED SIDE DOWN.

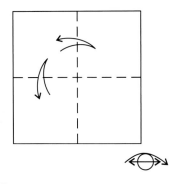

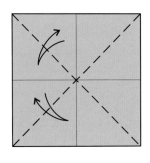

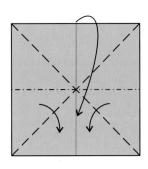

1) Fold and unfold the square in half lengthwise along both axes. Then turn the paper over left to right.

2) Fold and unfold the square in half diagonally along both axes.

3) Fold the upper section down and at the same time fold the sides in to make a waterbomb base.

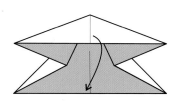

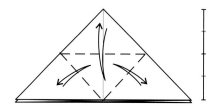

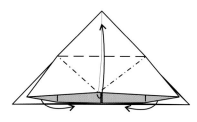

$\binom{4}{}$ Fold in progress.

$\binom{5}{}$ Fold the upper corner down and the lower corners up. Then unfold.

$\binom{6}{}$ Fold the upper layer up along the crease made previously. This will cause the sides to fold in.

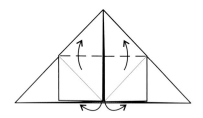

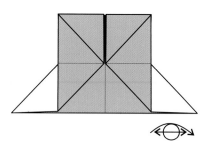

$\binom{7}{}$ Fold the upper layers up. This will cause the layer beneath to open up.

$\binom{8}{}$ Fold in progress. Then squash flat.

$\binom{9}{}$ Turn the model over left to right.

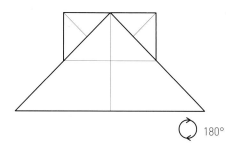

180°

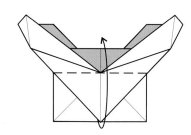

$\binom{10}{}$ Rotate the model by 180°.

$\binom{11}{}$ Fold the upper edge down from the middle crease. This will cause the adjacent sides to fold in.

$\binom{12}{}$ Fold both layers of the lower corner up.

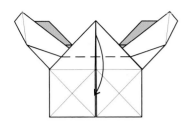

(13) Fold both layers of the triangle back down again.

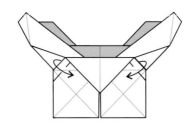

(14) Fold the edges in, beneath the middle folded triangle.

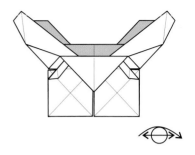

(15) Turn the model over left to right.

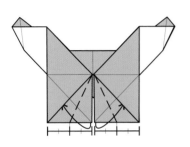

(16) Fold the inner of the lower corners over and tuck the corners into the adjacent pockets.

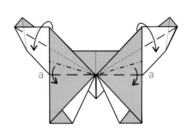

(17) Fold the upper layer down along (a–a). This will cause the paper above to slide over.

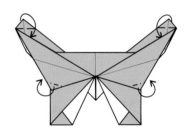

(18) Fold the tips of the 'wings' in. Then fold the lower corners of the middle section behind.

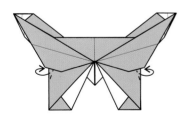

(19) Fold the outer corners behind to shape the wings.

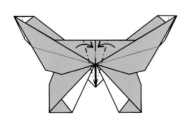

(20) Fold the centre of the 'body' in and then out to narrow it.

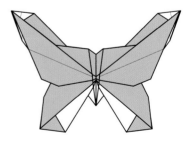

(21) Complete.

Frog

*

The frog is a classic design. The middle of the square becomes the tip of the nose, while the corners become the frog's legs. The final model can be inflated if you wish to add more volume to the body.

18 X 18CM (7 X 7IN)

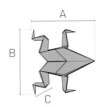

A 9.5cm (3¾in)
B 8.5cm (3⅓in)
C 2.5cm (1in)

START WITH A SQUARE, COLOURED SIDE UP AND FROM STEPS 1 TO 8
OF THE CLASSIC LILY (SEE PAGES 64-6).

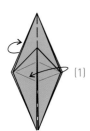

(1)

1 Fold one side over at the front and behind to expose the hidden faces.

2 Fold the edges in to the middle on all four sides.

3 Fold one side over front and behind.

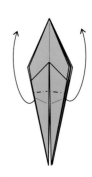

4 Reverse fold the legs inside.

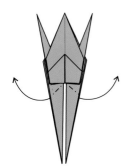

5 Reverse fold the lower legs to be perpendicular to the body.

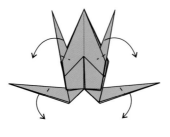

6 Reverse fold the points to shape the legs.

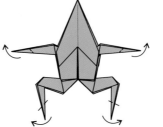

7 Reverse fold the ends of the legs to finish shaping the legs. Turn over.

8 Complete

Bird

**

The bird is folded to look as though it is sitting, perhaps on a branch or on the ground.
Try experimenting with models in complementary colours to create a group of birds.

18 X 18CM (7 X 7IN) x1

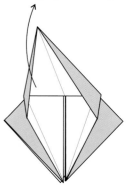

A 13.5cm (5⅓in)
B 2.5cm (1in)
C 2.5cm (1in)

START WITH A SQUARE, COLOURED SIDE UP.

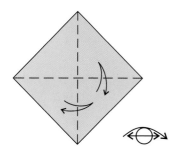

1. Fold and unfold the square in half diagonally along both axes. Then turn the paper over left to right.

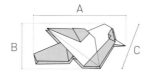

2. Fold and unfold the square in half lengthwise.

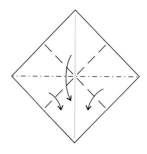

3. Fold the upper half down. At the same time fold in the sides making a preliminary base.

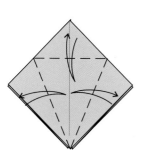

4. Fold and unfold the edges and the upper corner in.

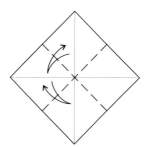

5. Fold the upper layer up along the horizontal fold made in the previous step, causing the edges to fold in.

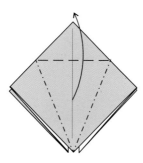

6. Fold in progress.

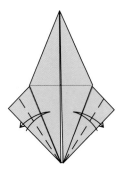

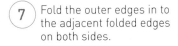

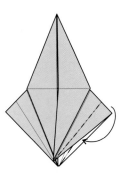

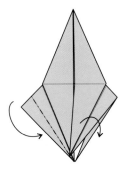

7 Fold the outer edges in to the adjacent folded edges on both sides.

8 Lift the point up and fold the edge inside along the crease made in the previous step.

9 Fold the point back down and repeat the process on the other side.

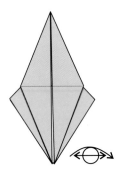

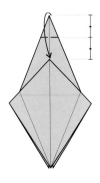

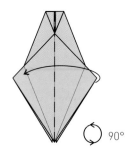

10 Turn the model over left to right.

11 Fold the upper corner down to the adjacent point.

12 Fold the model in half. Then rotate the model by 90°.

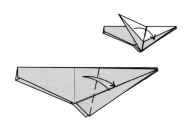

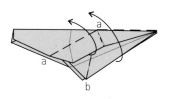

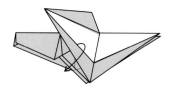

13 Fold and unfold the upper layer over to the right.

14 Fold the upper layer up to the left along the line (a–a). The lower layer should fold along (a–b). This will open the point.

15 Pull out the trapped paper and flatten.

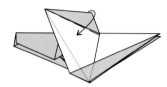

16 Fold the upper edge over.

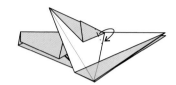

17 Fold the corner of the wing behind.

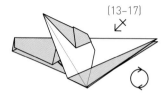

(13–17)

18 Repeat steps 13 to 17 on the reverse. Then rotate the model slightly.

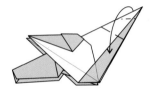

19 Fold the corner over.

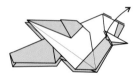

20 Unfold back to a point.

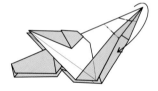

21 Reverse fold the point inside the model.

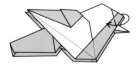

22 Fold the corner over on the front and behind.

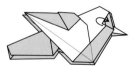

23 Fold the tip of the folded corner over on the front and behind to make eyes.

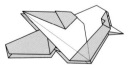

24 Complete.

Snail
✳✳

The snail works because of its simple construction, its shell formed by a triangle. Character is added by means of the head tentacles, which give a sense of fun to the final model.

18 X 18CM (7 X 7IN)

x1

A
B
C

A 12cm (4¾in)
B 8cm (3⅓in)
C 2cm (¾in)

START WITH A SQUARE, COLOURED SIDE UP.

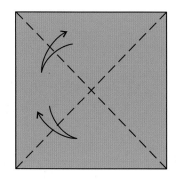

(1) Fold and unfold the square in half diagonally along both axes. Then turn the paper over left to right.

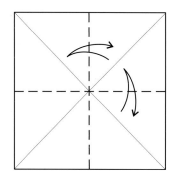

(2) Fold and unfold the square in half lengthwise along both axes.

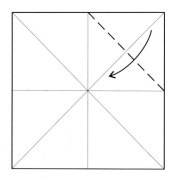

(3) Fold the upper right corner in to the middle of the paper.

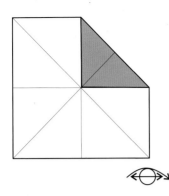

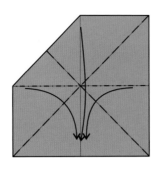

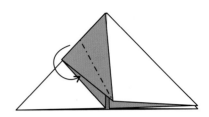

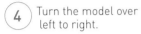

4) Turn the model over left to right.

5) Fold the corners in and refold the creases made previously to make a waterbomb base with one corner folded in.

6) Reverse fold the left edge of the folded-in corner into the triangle.

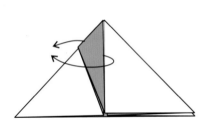

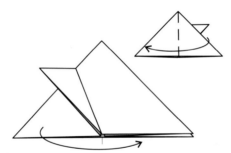

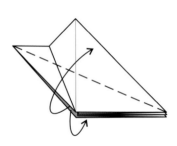

7) Turn the paper on the outer layer inside out and reverse the trapped paper.

8) Fold the rear corner behind so that three points are facing to the right.

9) Fold the edges up on the front layer and behind.

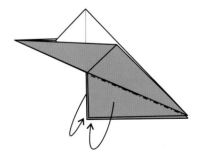

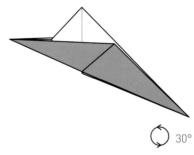

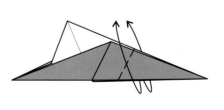

10) Fold the lower edges of the inner section inside the model.

11) Rotate the model anticlockwise by 30°.

12) Fold the right point up and turn it inside out.

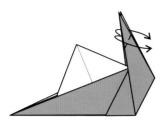

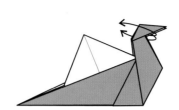

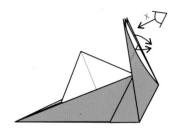

(13) Turn the point inside out.

(14) Unfold the reverse-folded point.

(15) Reverse fold the inner section of the point.

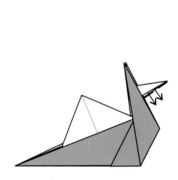

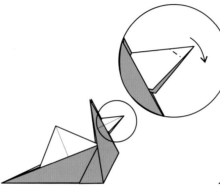

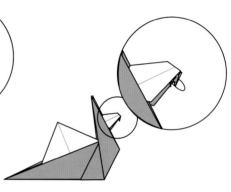

(16) Fold out the paper inside the folded point.

(17) Reverse fold the tip of the point.

(18) Fold the corner into the 'head'.

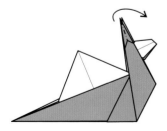

(19) Pinch the upper points together on both sides to form the tentacles.

(20) Curve the tentacles and open the base of the model slightly. If it doesn't stand up, slide the neck back slightly.

(21) Complete.

RESOURCES AND ACKNOWLEDGEMENTS

AUTHOR'S WEBSITE
Creaselightning
www.creaselightning.co.uk
Mark Bolitho's website featuring his work.

ORIGAMI SOCIETIES
Asociación Española de Papiroflexia (Spain)
www.pajarita.org
Spanish origami society

British Origami Society (UK)
www.britishorigami.org.uk
One of the most established origami societies.

CDO (Italy)
www.origami-cdo.it
Italian origami society

Japan Origami Academic Society (Japan)
Origami.gr.jp
Japanese origami association with a good magazine on advanced folding techniques.

MEPP (France)
www.mfpp-origami.fr
French origami society

Nippon Origami Association (Japan)
www.origami-noa.jp
Japanese origami society

Origami Australia
www.origami.org.au
Australian origami society

Origami Deutschland
www.papierfalten.de
German origami society

Origami USA
www.origamiusa.org
With headquarters in New York, this society holds one of the biggest origami conventions of the year.

OTHER ORGANIZATIONS
Colour Tree Ltd (UK)
www.colortreelimited.co.uk
Good supplies of origami papers.

European Origami Museum (Spain)
www.emoz.es
An origami museum in Zaragoza, Spain

John Gerard Paper studios (Germany)
www.gerard-paperworks.com
Paper makers with a range of handmade papers.

Origami Spirit (USA)
www.origamispirit.com
Origami blog and a range of interesting projects.

Origamido Studios (USA)
www.origamido.com
A paper art studio that also produces bespoke paper for origami artists.

Shepherds Falkiners Fine Paper UK
www.store.bookbinding.co.uk
UK-based supplier of fine papers.

AUTHOR'S ACKNOWLEDGEMENTS
Thanks to Marion, John, Simon, Beth, Luke, Alex, Talia, Nick, Jen, Annabelle, Jack, Olly and Graham, and to my friends and family for their support in my origami journey.